If You Love Someone, You Must Tell Them

NEAL ALLEN

Copyright © 2023 Neal Allen
All rights reserved
First Edition

PAGE PUBLISHING
Conneaut Lake, PA

First originally published by Page Publishing 2023

ISBN 979-8-88793-048-0 (pbk)
ISBN 979-8-88793-053-4 (digital)

Printed in the United States of America

To the families of Christopher and Lavinia Gelineau and to the soldiers and families of the Maine National Guard.

Contents

Introduction vii

Book One
Chapter 1:   September 9, 2001: Peabody Pond 1
Chapter 2:   Running Red Lights 3
Chapter 3:   Lavinia and Chris 8

Book Two
Chapter 4:   September 11, 2001 26
Chapter 5:   Afghanistan: Operation Enduring Freedom 43
Chapter 6:   Operation Iraqi Freedom 50
Chapter 7:   The 133rd Deployed to Iraq 72
Chapter 8:   April 20, 2004: The Convoy 92

Book Three
Chapter 9:   Commencement 115
Chapter 10: If You Love Someone, You Must Tell Them 121
Chapter 11: April 9, 2005: Reunited 174

Postscript: heading to Romania 176

Notes and Sources 187

Bibliography 189

Acknowledgments 191

Introduction

As the Twin Towers collapsed, the life stories of many took a sudden turn. *Nine eleven*, two words that sound as one, immediately trigger instant replay memories, of where we were and what we were doing. The sheer physical and emotional force of that day ignited an avalanche of unintended consequences. For many, life's compass was no longer fixed on True North as the magnetic field of public outrage and political power reset the needle.

If You Love Someone, You Must Tell Them is a true story that profiles a young woman from Romania who meets a young man from Vermont. The magic spark of young love when first discovered connects the two as one. While the unintended consequences of their individual decisions bring Lavinia and Christopher together, there is no escape from the larger world to which they have joined. That world is a complicated, busy intersection and to successfully navigate, takes skill, timing, and more than a small measure of good luck.

I first came to know Lavinia Onitiu in 2002, through an internship that I was pleased to offer her in my capacity as executive director of the Greater Portland Council of Governments. With an enthusiastic recommendation of our staff, it was quickly apparent that Lavinia was an exceedingly bright, multilingual student. During that period, I also had the pleasure to meet her boyfriend, Christopher D. Gelineau, a computer whiz with a smile as contagious as Lavinia's. On the occasion of meeting Chris, I encouraged him to provide me with his résumé; and by the next morning, it was on my desk.

Central to the story of Chris and Lavinia is the Iraq mission that Chris was a part of. Along with the other 570 men and women of Maine's 133rd, Army National Guard Engineering Battalion, Chris deployed to Iraq in early 2004. The battalion's destination was Mosul, Iraq's second-largest city, located 250 miles north of Baghdad.

That the National Guard was deployed for an active role in the war speaks to the larger political military decisions that were made in the post-Vietnam era of the 1980s. Even the hint of a return to a military draft would be a doomed proposition. For that and other reasons, troop strength policy shifted to the blending of National Guard and Reserve units with the regular military in certain situations. The policy was first implemented during the Gulf War of the early nineties in which 17 percent of the force was drawn from National Guard and Reserve units. That number exceeded over 45 percent during the Iraq War military mission.

The dual mission of the 133rd was to provide military and humanitarian support to the *Operation Iraqi Freedom* initiative. Under the steady, competent leadership of the battalion's commander, John Jansen, the responsibilities and reach of the 133rd covered an area equivalent in size to a region stretching from Philadelphia to Boston.

Regardless of one's opinion of the Iraq War, both in battle and community building, the 133rd served with distinction, integrity, and a commitment to excellence. Their performance was exemplary and represents the best of the American military and the quality and work ethic that define Maine and its people.

Beginning with Jansen and John William "Bill" Libby, who at that time was serving as the adjutant general of the Maine National Guard, my interactions with the soldiers of the 133rd make this book possible. Their support and input, including sharing of memories and at times, the embedded emotional scars of living twenty-four seven in a war-zone environment, has been a moving and personally transformative chapter in my life.

The military focus of the book begins with the September 11, 2001, chapter. Included in that chapter are *where-were-you*-type interviews with soldiers of the 133rd and others whom I interviewed.

With the caveat that the book is not a deep-dive, academic analysis of the Iraq War, the story of Chris and Lavinia would be incomplete without establishing some historical context and perspective of the war. To that end, the interviews, Internet research, media reports, and the writings of other authors were indispensable sources of relevant information and perspective.

On the next to the last page of former President George W. Bush's book, *Decision Points*, he writes, "As I hope I've made clear, I believe I got some of those decisions right, and I got some wrong. But on every one, I did what I believed was in the best interests of our country." He goes on to say, "It's too early to say how most of my decisions will turn out."

With respect to the war in Iraq, Bush is correct. It is too early to say in the long term. In present time, the scorecard is a mixed bag. A new Constitution, built on the parliamentary system, was approved by the voters in 2005, and subsequent elections have been held. However, voter participation has dropped dramatically over the first fifteen years since the Constitution was adopted.

Of further significance to the future of Iraq, the Parliamentary elections of 2021 resulted in the inability of the various parties to form a consensus government as required under their Constitution. The political dysfunction, including associated deadly violence, continues to plague the country. As I write this, there are signs of progress, but Iraq will not succeed if future elections are marked by stalling tactics, violence, and lengthy delays in the peaceful transfer of power.

With the world's fifth largest crude oil reserves and two significant rivers—the Tigris and Euphrates—that flow across the country and into the Persian Gulf, Iraq is positioned to build a long-term, sustainable economy. But to reach that point, it must find a way to come together. Eventually the government, as with any government on the planet, cannot function without a workable political system that consistently provides predictable funding and security on the streets.

Returning to Bush's rhetorical question, it is conceivable but too early to predict that the U.S.-led invasion may one day be considered a key turning point in transforming Iraq into a more open and politically stable nation. That's the optimistic, glass-is-half-full hope, and if the country achieves long-term stability, it will be the future generations who will not only read about it as history but will also be the beneficiaries.

In contemporary times, though, the impacts of the war have been staggering when tallied up by the deaths and injuries of civilians and soldiers, PTSD survivors, suicides, and broken lives that never mended and the trillions of dollars poured in to the cause. And because the Iraq War is viewed by many as a war of choice, its legacy for those who have lived through these years and especially those who lost loved ones is the repeating echo of Lavinia's rhetorical cry, "Why is this war?"

A positive that would add a measure of value but can never morally justify the staggering numbers who died and the enormous destruction would be the emergence of Iraq as a politically and economically stable nation at peace.

After the U.S. military withdrew from Iraq in 2011, they returned three years later to assist the Iraqi Security Forces (ISF) in response to the atrocities of the Islamic State of Iraq and Syria (ISIS). While the combined efforts of the ISF and US forces were eventually successful in regaining control of the territories that ISIS had seized, the potential for continued acts of terrorism remains. Driven by the invitation of the Iraq government, 2,500 U.S. troops continue to serve in a training and advisory role while creating a low but important presence.

The question of what motivated me to write this book connects to a core belief that history is fundamentally unique and important to the human experience. Just as all politics is local, the genesis of history is likewise and can be both interesting and instructive if we pay attention. In parallel with that proposition, I find history to take on greater relevancy when presented through the lives of individuals and not just those who achieve "fame." Biography and autobiography personalize and provide context to the larger moments and events that define us as a people and the times in which we live.

Setting aside the textbook focus on memorizing specific dates and the names of famous leaders, there is a story within each of us that is often deeper and more revealing than might be expected at first glance. Rarely, though, do we think of our lives as a part of history. But the story of our times and generations before and yet to come is a complicated, patchwork quilt that we are all part of. Behind individual fame, there are many who enable its success or failure.

Every book reflects a structure through which the author decides to frame the story. I struggled with the challenge of how to connect the pieces of this book into a logical narrative.

While I will leave it to those who read and critique whether I was successful, I stepped back and reflected on how I tend to read a book. If the genre is fiction and it holds my attention, the book compels a cover-to-cover read. Confession, with the exception of biography, I rarely read a nonfiction book in its entirety. I take from it what is of interest, knowing that I can return to the book at any time.

Drawing on my reading habits as a guide, I defaulted to a structure that organizes the chapters in three separate *books* plus a more personal *postscript*, "Heading to Romania." Each book is designed to be read and hopefully appreciated as a stand-alone, short story. Optimistically, I believe that some of the chapters may also be read and appreciated in much the same way. Whether that holds true is far beyond my control, but I share that opinion in order to inform the reader of my intent.

Thus, the unifying elements of each book include relevant references to Lavinia and Chris, together with the overarching event of 9/11, all wrapped around the universal theme of unintended consequences.

In my attempt to capture, if even partially, the story of Lavinia and Chris, the input and memories of their family, friends, and members of the Maine National Guard and its 133rd Engineering Battalion were invaluable. Drawing from these sources and select emails and writings of Lavinia provides compelling insight and authenticity of her many gifts, her inspiring humanity, and the natural ease that connected her and Chris together as one.

The decision to write a book—this book—was a uniquely self-imposed challenge. Whatever success I may have achieved during my decades-long career in public management was due in no small part to embracing consensus and collaboration as a guiding principle.

When I decided to write this book, I soon came to realize that collaboration and consensus would be driven from within. It was no longer a group decision. It was uniquely my decision, and to that end, I asked myself two fundamental questions. Do I want to write the story? And do I believe in the purpose of writing the story?

While the idea of writing a book was daunting and frankly more than a tad out of my comfort zone, my answer to both questions was a resounding yes. I also recognized that the corollary of those guiding principles is a commitment to be patient and willing to invest the time to reach the finish line. For me, I also found that concentrated writing became such a deep, personal process that other parts of my life were unintentionally zoned out.

Like an artist who may take months or years, to add the final, subtle stroke before signing the canvas, an author may consume months or years rewriting paragraphs, pages, adding content, or reducing content before tapping the "save" key for the final time. I have crossed that finish line, and it was more of a marathon than a sprint.

Chapter 1

September 9, 2001
Peabody Pond

September in Maine is the best of the best. The days are warm and sunny with soft, comforting breezes. The nights carry a chill of what awaits but is otherwise perfect for sleep, ushered in by the reassuring symphony of chirping male crickets as their plea for the silent female crickets grows louder, only to one nightfall silent.

The tiny but always persistent blackflies have faded away since their rebellious swarms of spring, and the always menacing mosquitos are on the run, thanks in part to the brilliantly designed helicopter dragonflies as they dart and devour their prey. The progression of our insect friends through the spring and summer months reminds us of the inevitable cycle of the seasons. While it is often difficult to rationalize the purpose of some of these creatures, deep down, I understand that like all life-forms, they, too, have a role to play in the chain we share. Selfishly, I wish they would leave me alone. But to their credit, there is no singular bias. We are all equal-opportunity targets.

Peabody Pond[1] is the product of the Ice Age many thousands of years ago. Modest in size at two miles long and sixty-four feet deep, Peabody is a gem that forms part of the Sebago Lake watershed region. With numerous giant boulders scattered randomly above and just below the surface left abandoned in the wake of receding ice, Peabody is best suited for kayaks and canoes. Its waters are clear and cool, and against the backdrop of northern New England mountains and forests, there are moments when the only sound is the unmistakable, primeval cry of a loon.

The Sunday of September 9, 2001, was as perfect a day as one will ever experience. Midseventies with full sun, only a whisper of a cloud in the sky. After Labor Day, with camps closed down, family vacations over, and kids back in school, there is a naturally quiet change of pace as "normal" life begins anew with its steady but predictable routine. In Maine, the seasons are clearly defined markers to the annual beat of time.

Set between the Maine towns of Sebago, Naples, and Bridgton, Peabody Pond seems the very definition of peaceful. No other boats of any kind or people, for that matter, can be seen or heard. I turned toward Jill in the other kayak and said, "*This is too perfect. Something is going to happen.*"

---

[1] Lakes Environmental Association, mainelakes.org. *Peabody Pond* (Bridgton, Maine, 2022).

Chapter 2

Running Red Lights

While we assume each day will follow a predictable pattern that begins with our commute to work and ends with a safe return home, intuition aside, there is no crystal ball-warning that if we make a split-second decision to run a red light, the day may forever be marked by death, paralysis, or time in prison for vehicular manslaughter. Life is that fragile. We only forget the split-second decision if nothing happens. Otherwise, that split-second decision shadows us for the rest of our lives.

By making the spontaneous decision to run the light, we are changing the equation of our normal routine by including a circumstance of higher risk. We make that split-second decision, confident that we will successfully clear the intersection, thereby saving many precious seconds while waiting for the light to turn green. Measured by any cost-benefit standard this is a stupid and selfish, unheroic decision, carrying enormous life-changing risks for ourselves and innocent others.

We all know that the "big" decisions—where to live, work, and with whom—will carry us in new and different directions. That is why we make those decisions. Each separately will likely determine the other two. And while we hope that the desired outcomes will be realized, the playing field of life is a constantly shifting dynamic that can just as easily bring us to a result that is the polar opposite of what we intended.

Thus, we accept as routine the countless decisions, which we know from experience carry a predictable outcome. On a few occasions, the pattern is broken through an unanticipated event that affects us directly. While such events may morph into something much larger, they are usually nothing more than one of the many minor inconveniences of life in twenty-first-century America—a dead car battery, a sick child at school, a late meeting. Inconvenient, for sure, but manageable and unlikely to be life altering.

Every so often, the events are huge and beyond our individual ability to manage. On a broad, universal scale, consider those who chose to take a personal day off on September 11, 2001, from their job at the World Trade Center. It is unlikely that such a decision was driven by a mysterious force of warning but rather, the result of a relatively minor personal circumstance.

Whatever the reason, it would be a brief matter of time before the consequences of taking that day off would be grasped with a chilling and dark realization that friends, colleagues, and others were trapped in what must have been an eternal moment of pure hell.

Through a simple decision to not work that day or a minor, unexpected delay, some were spared from that inferno but certainly not spared from the life-changing emotions of losing friends and colleagues and realizing what might have been.

For many, such events result in recurring feelings of survivor guilt—a documented condition soldiers feel and at the very extreme, survivors of horrific events, such as the *Holocaust*. We can now tragically include the prospect of survivor guilt that will plague Ukrainians as a result of Russian President Vladimir Putin's unprovoked and illegal attack that has included the deliberate bombing of hospitals, apartments, and the murder of innocent children, women, and men. Many Russian soldiers forced to fight will feel the guilt of their deeds. The emotional, psychological trauma of war impacts the defenders and the invaders.

Also consider the innocent passengers and crew of the four hijacked airplanes and reflect on the sudden horror they must have felt when realizing that their decision to fly on this day, at this time, and on this specific flight was life ending. To the first responders and particularly the heroic firefighters who clearly understood the risks of entering the Twin Towers, their day started in its customary, routine manner with no premonition of airplanes flying into buildings. The only red lights they ran were to get to the scene. Those first responders were simply doing what they were trained to do, being prepared and responding to whatever the situation required.

Just as our daily decisions, be they deliberate or circumstantial, can bring tragic, unintended consequences, the flip side to that proposition can be a deeply enriching and life-altering moment. The unknown interactions that occur through chance meetings and even tragic events have resulted in many a romantic relationship, lifetime friendship, or career-altering encounter. These are the unanticipated fruits that bring truth to the beauty of life and the unfathomable probability that we are even here at all.

Other than the motivation to live and survive, our interactions with others are among the most consequential choices that we make. Included in that wider stage of life are the individual decisions we make that cumulatively impact the whole. In our democracy, nowhere is this more impactful on our lives than in the election of our political leaders to whom we bestow the responsibility to govern.

The right to vote is a privilege that too many of our fellow citizens ironically fail to exercise. Absent system-wide barriers to voting, the lame excuse that my vote won't change anything, or that elections don't matter is ignorant and arrogant. Ignorant because the eligible nonvoter can only see his or her vote in isolation. The decision to not vote is arrogant because it demeans a right and privilege that has been denied to millions throughout the world, both past and present, including citizens of the United States.

We will never know whether the statistically deadlocked vote for president in 2000 that was settled by the United States Supreme Court (Bush versus Gore) in a 5–4 decision,[1] thereby electing George W. Bush as president, triggered a chain reaction of events that kept the American military fighting in Afghanistan and Iraq for two decades.

This leads back to the story of Lavinia and Chris, and it's fair to ask, would the 9/11 attacks even have taken place under an Al Gore Presidency? While the question is speculative, a Gore administration would have been built around a team of civilian and military leaders with different backgrounds and perspectives from the team under Bush.

Assuming, though, that the attacks had occurred during a Gore Presidency, it seems likely that America's response to root out the terrorist cells in Afghanistan would have been similar to what Bush authorized. The larger question remains and will forever remain unanswered: Would President Gore have authorized invading Iraq, a country that was not directly connected to the 9/11 attacks? If so, would the more traditional role of the National Guard shift to the extent that it did under President Bush from the home front to the battlefronts of Afghanistan and Iraq?

In truth, there is no definitive answer to such questions, but they underscore the important responsibility to participate, read, listen, and ask questions. Elections have consequences on both the good and bad sides of the ledger. The constitutional responsibility of authorizing and activating the use of military force falls on the civilian-led commander-in-chief, the president of the United States and the United States Congress. And over the seven-decade, post–World War II era, America's presidents on both sides of the aisle have often been the most vocal advocates for using the military to settle issues.

Presidents and a relatively small few who serve at his or her pleasure determine where and when to use military power. It is an awesome responsibility that ultimately falls on the shoulders of thousands of men and women with names we only learn when they are killed.

The question haunts: Do our leaders who decide the where and when to deploy America's huge military power do so only after *all* potential consequences of that action have been thoroughly filtered and vetted? Or instead, do they rationalize the use of force on a calculation similar to running a red light? That the intersection looks clear, and therefore, the decision to "go in" carries a predictable and expedient outcome. What could possibly go wrong? The answer to that question is the stuff of history which spins on the law of unintended consequences.

IF YOU LOVE SOMEONE, YOU MUST TELL THEM

With the final hour of September 11 turning to the first hour of September 12, America and the world awakened to the new day with the realization that a dramatic page of history was being written. No one knew where it would lead, but as with all such momentous events, there would be unanticipated consequences.

Playing the odds on any given day, I assume that my day will end with the promise of a new day. Contrast my reality to that of the millions who struggle to survive each twenty-four-hour cycle in constant fear for themselves and their families. Their decisions and slender options for making it to another day are at a level I can only imagine. While it is well to remember that we each live our lives in the context of our circumstances, my circumstances are a luxury when viewed through the world of a mother or father or orphaned child surviving each day in a war-torn zone or trapped in a depressed, low-income neighborhood.

The story of Lavinia and Chris is a story of love and life and carries a reminder that no matter how much we plan and dream and feel comfortable with our decisions, the road we take will lead us to both anticipated and unanticipated events and the consequences on both the good and bad side of that equation. In that context, may we never be so arrogant as to forget that the common denominator defining the peoples of the world is the will to survive, love, and wake up to a new sunrise.

---

[1] *Bush Versus Gore*, 5331 US 98 (2000), was a landmark decision of the United States Supreme Court on December 12, 2000, that reversed an order by the Florida Supreme Court for a selective manual recount of that state's United States presidential election ballots. The 5–4 decision effectively awarded Florida's twenty-five Electoral College votes to Republican candidate George W. Bush, thereby ensuring victory over Democratic candidate Al Gore.

Chapter 3

Lavinia and Chris

ONCE THEY MET, IT WAS CLEAR THAT Lavinia and Chris had awakened to the realization, that together, there was a higher life to experience, both professionally and personally. To reach that place, they were motivated by their economic and life circumstances to use the system that defined their reality, and both understood that the cornerstone of that system was education. To excel on that path would open the door to the wider world of new choices, new adventures, and new friends.

Lavi's strengths, of which there were many, flowed from her pure love of learning and in particular, languages and literature. Chris had the passion, aptitude, and gift to excel in the evolving technologies of our time. Their tickets to a promising future were scholarships for Lavi and the National Guard for Chris. The Guard was a twofer: service to community and country and a supporting revenue stream to help with education expenses. These were the choices made before they met that set them on a course to the University of Southern Maine where their paths intersected.

Although the name *Lavinia* is not widely used, it evokes a unique and gracious feel. For all who met Lavinia, these are descriptives that fit perfectly with their first and lasting impressions of her. Complementing the beauty and charm was a woman of compassion, determination, and substance.

Lavi, as she preferred to be called, was born on October 16, 1979, in the City of Sibiu, Romania. Her first decade of life was during the last decade of communist rule in Romania under the brutal dictator Nicolae Ceausescu. She and her brother, Marius, lived with their parents on the third floor of a large multistory apartment building overlooking a busy Sibiu street. Life was a balance between her unwavering commitment to learning and helping with family chores, including the care and harvesting of potatoes on a small family-owned plot of land a few miles from the city.

More times than not, the love and guidance of one parent is all that is needed for a child to take the right path in life. For Lavi, it was her mother, Iulia, who was there each and every day with love, support, and guidance. The mother-daughter bond was unbreakable and enduring with Iulia always encouraging Lavi to reach for the stars and pursue her dreams, whatever they may be and wherever they may take her.

Lavi's passion to learn burned at an early age, and as described by Iulia, when she was a student at *Lucian Blaga University* in Sibiu, many hours were spent at the library working on her English and reading and immersing herself in Shakespeare and other great literature. According to Iulia, on one occasion, the librarian commented that it was okay to be doing other things, to which Lavi responded that being at the library was exactly where she wanted to be. Such was her intellectual curiosity and motivation to reach for the stars.

As a beautiful young woman with a vibrant, open personality, Lavi could easily have cultivated an active social life during her late teen and young adult years. Whether it was writing poetry or composing music that she would sing while playing her guitar, Lavi's creative, artistic side brimmed with an honest energy that found a peaceful and protective home in the quiet corners of the library. In that context, it is easy to understand how pursuing an active social life was secondary to her intellectual curiosity and the power of learning. The library complemented her commitment to learning and kindled a realization that education would be the ticket to a much different and more stimulating life.

While Lavi was not one to be easily intimidated and by all accounts, thrived on competitive academic challenge, the library also offered a wider and more personal window to the world, as it was figuratively and literally an "open book" for her to use in designing a lifetime-learning process. In that setting, Lavi was her own teacher, motivated by a self-imposed discipline that has defined so many accomplished women and men throughout history.

During Lavi's last year at *Octavian Goga* High School, she was required to take an equivalency exam, or baccalaureate as it was called. The exam covered a range of subjects, and Lavi scored second among all of Sibiu County. With this achievement, Lavi was awarded a scholarship to attend *Lucian Blaga University* in Sibiu where she completed her first two years of college.

Without the financial support of that scholarship, Lavi would have been unable to attend college, although one has to believe that given her passion to learn, she would have found a way. Not surprisingly, her area of concentration was English and French languages. Through a combination of her language skills, brilliant academic record, and advanced study of Shakespeare, Lavi was invited to attend an academic conference in Sibiu at the university and to serve as a translator.

Leading educators from around the world were attending the conference, and through pure chance, Lavi ended up sitting next to a senior male official of the University of Maine. In recalling this event, Iulia is unable to remember the name of that person but clearly recalls being told how impressed he was with Lavi's advanced knowledge of Shakespeare. Through that contact, Lavi was encouraged to seek a scholarship to the University of Maine system with a recommendation that the University of Southern Maine, with its urban setting in Portland, would be the best fit.

Lavi's exemplary academic record together with strong recommendations from her college professors provided a compelling application in support of a scholarship to attend the University of Southern Maine. As the world rolled into the year 2000, Lavi was thrilled to receive notice that she was indeed heading to the United States as the recipient of a scholarship to attend the University of Southern Maine.

*****

Generous of spirit and giving unselfishly of his time, Chris Gelineau was among that small group who are always ready and willing to help others regardless of any personal inconvenience. Instead of frowning and rolling his eyes, clear signals by some that they are too busy or really not interested enough to lend a hand, Chris would jump in with a broad and welcoming smile. Helping others gave purpose to life and if there was a problem to be solved, especially in the mysterious world of information technology, all the more challenging. Chris was a computer geek without being a nerd.

Chris's road to Bristol, Vermont, began in Houston, Texas, on October 23, 1980, the day he was born at St. Luke's Children's Hospital. His parents, John and Vicky Gelineau, had moved from Vermont for the stronger job market in Houston. John Gelineau recalls the difficult birth that brought Chris into the world with the umbilical cord wrapped around his neck. He was blue and went into cardiac arrest, prompting an emergency team of doctors to immediately and successfully respond.

Two years later when the couple separated, John returned to Burlington. Vicky and Chris would follow him soon thereafter, settling in nearby Colchester. Vicky eventually remarried and together with Chris, moved to Oklahoma where her husband, Jesse Chicoine, was serving in the Air Force. They remained in Oklahoma for a few years, but when Chicoine chose to not reenlist, they moved back to Vermont.

Believing it would be important for Chris to develop physically, Vicky enrolled him in a martial arts school. According to John Gelineau, Chris was not aware that his uncle, Paul Gelineau, was a black belt teacher of Judo and at that time, was teaching young students like Chris in his class. Through his uncle, Chris learned not only the skills of Judo but the martial arts mindset to never be the aggressor in the heat of moment. Only use the discipline and skills to defend oneself. John Gelineau believes that "it was during these years that Chris began to develop his confident but quiet personality."

It is said that knowledge is power, and as the twentieth century gave way to the twenty-first, there was no pause to the dramatic evolution of sophisticated, cutting-edge information technology. Clearly, a special status was crowned on those who effortlessly navigated the new, revolutionary technologies of our time. The young seemed to be born with a computer chip embedded in their brain.

Excepting for the hardened cynics who refused to go near a computer, folks like me looked on with awe at people like Chris who, in a matter of seconds, could tap a few keys and magically solve a problem or up would pop a supercool feature that we neophytes had never seen. In contrast, my genius solution to a computer glitch was to randomly tap as many keys as my fingers could touch in a five-second burst of frustration. Not surprisingly, it never ended well.

At least as it applies to the early generations of information technology, the advent of the computer age ushered in one of history's more unanticipated and ironic adjustments to the household balance of power. Young, nourished, and evolving brains could take to computers as quickly as they learn the alphabet. And while parents still helped their kids with homework, it was those very same kids that parents often turned to for help in understanding and operating their computers.

Generational shortcomings aside, the mystery and sheer excitement of the information technology age was quick to lure Chris Gelineau into its *World Wide Web*. Similar to Lavi's passion for languages and long hours in the library, Chris's passion for computers compelled him to join the computer club at Mt. Abraham High School.

When he was not driving around Bristol delivering pizzas for Cubber's, with high school friend Justin Bouvier, Chris could be found in the Mt. Abe computer lab. He thrived in that lab, learning the details of programming and how to write code. Being ahead of one's peers on the ways and means of using technology helped to shape the self-confident ease that defined Chris's personality as a young adult. Knowledge after all is power.

During this period, Chris developed a special friendship of the "best-friend" kind. Most friendships begin through some kind of random situation or connection, and it was no different for Chris when he met Travis Scribner. Having just moved from Winooski, Vermont, to the Bristol, Vermont area, Chris was entering the ninth grade.

Scribner described how Chris was sitting behind him in English class, and realizing that he needed a pencil, he turned and said, "Hey, new kid, got a pencil I could have?" And thus, a "great friendship" was started, a friendship that blossomed through high school. Chris and Travis spent long hours together, and as described by Scribner, Chris "quickly became part of the family." Scribner's mother attributed the acceptance of Chris in to their home by how "genuine" he was.[1]

Over those high school years, his friendship with Scribner evolved to include Travis's high school sweetheart, Leslie, as a good friend. In fact, of the many good times, Scribner recalls the 1998 ice storm and how he and Chris were stranded at Leslie's house for three days. They whiled away the time playing board games and drinking hot cocoa. Later that year when Scribner was away at basic training, it was Chris who was there as a friend to support Leslie.

Senior Year, Mt. Abraham High School, Bristol, Vermont

When Chris graduated with honors from Mount Abraham High School in 1999, it was clear that he would build a career in computers and information technology. But to ride that wave as far as possible, Chris was smart enough to know that there was much still to learn. And to reach that higher level, it would cost more money than available family resources and delivering pizzas could provide.

Chris's message to Leslie in their 1999 yearbook speaks to those adolescent years of self-discovery and growth.

> Hey Leslie. We're finally done! Now on to bigger and better things. We've been through a lot of things, and I don't know where I am going with this. I am glad that we became friends way back when. I'm glad that we are still friends! When I come back and when Travis comes back we all have to hang out sometimes. Like what I always say before: Catch ya later. Chris

Happy Summer Days in Vermont

Together in Portland

Not only did they hang out but the strength of the special friendship between Chris and Travis was later affirmed in a most personal way, with each serving as the other's best man.

September 11, 2001, was just another blank date on a future calendar.

Joining the National Guard

Following the footsteps of his best friend, Travis Scribner, Chris joined the Vermont National Guard (131st Engineers) in 1998. One year later, after graduating from high school, he was off to South Carolina for basic training. John Gelineau remembers the special time that he and Chris shared traveling back to Vermont at the end of basic training and how that time and those miles were used by Chris to learn the special skills of driving a stick shift.

Like many others who made such a choice in the pre-9/11 1990s, Chris assumed that the role of the National Guard as first responders would continue a focus on natural disasters, civil unrest, and special community betterment projects. And like Chris, many enlistees came from families with limited resources, but also like Chris, the men and women joining the National Guard shared common aspirations for higher education. Join the Guard and draw the benefits of an income stream and scholarship opportunities while serving one's country.

Excelling at a high level and experiencing the positive reinforcement of others builds self-esteem, confidence, and a sense of stature. And those qualities served to define who Chris was becoming when he transferred in 2000 from the Vermont National Guard to the Maine Army Reserve National Guard to begin his studies in the *technology and information management* department at the University of Southern Maine.

Wherever Chris landed, it was only a brief period before his skills were in demand. Beginning in high school with his programming work and continuing at USM where he created websites for university departments, Chris became known as a go-to guy for solving complex technology problems and always with patience, dedication, and good humor.

Chris was creative, and when he could blend his technology prowess with some good-natured fun, he would not let the opportunity pass. A fellow solider and USM classmate, Franz Oberlerchner, recalled an event that did just that, "While we were training at Fort Drum in New York, and had a night of beers and goofing off, someone did something funny that I saw Chris catch on film. I made a passing comment that I would love to have a copy of it. Chris had been listening because the next morning he brought a CD copy to formation for me."[2]

Another fellow soldier, Major Ben Leonard, also began his military career as Chris had in 1999 when he joined the Vermont National Guard. And like Chris, Leonard enrolled in the University of Southern Maine while transferring to the Maine National Guard in 2000. Given the common connections, Leonard became a close friend to both Chris and Lavi. Following his completion of the University of New Hampshire's ROTC program in 2005, he transferred to the New Hampshire Army Reserve National Guard. In June of 2018, I met Ben for lunch in Portsmouth, New Hampshire, where he now serves in a full-time capacity in the NHARNG, holding the rank of major. Describing Chris as "brilliant in the field of IT," Leonard added, "Chris was quiet but always there to help, and very smart just like, Lavinia."[3]

Arriving on the University of Southern Maine campus in the fall of 2000

Lavi became best of friends with Denitza Dimitrova, a sophomore student from Bulgaria who described Lavi as "the kind of girl who lights up the room, who carries sunshine, and who makes a great first impression without even trying."[4]. At that time, Lavi's brother, Marius, was studying computer science at the University of Maine's flagship campus in Orono and would occasionally travel to Portland from Orono to visit.

Dimitrova had recently been selected to serve as a first year mentor at USM's most diverse housing facility, Portland Hall, in downtown Portland. A younger international student from Palestine introduced Lavi to Dimitrova, describing her as a "very outgoing, friendly, and constantly smiling girl from Romania."

Dimitrova writes:

> Lavinia was really easy to talk to. We had so much in common…becoming friends with Lavi came so naturally. We were alike in many ways—we were both very open people, we came from similar cultures and experienced the same difficulties while adapting to a new culture. She struck me as very intelligent and friendly. I felt like I rarely met people as cultured as she was. What I always admired in Lavi's behavior was that she was never worried that she would sound or appear foolish, which often happens to foreigners in a new culture. Every time we cooked or had meals together, we told each other words for foods in our native languages, which we thought might be similar in Bulgarian and Romanian, and they usually were. Every word that matched in both languages brought us so much excitement. As if it were something important, something worth being happy about. Blissful carefree times.

Not knowing exactly where her education may lead and typical of Lavi to keep her options open, she took on the extra challenge of a double major. On the humanities side, it was English and French, and on the more professionally focused careers, her choice was business. Not surprisingly, her commitment to learning brought the same level of intensity and highest academic achievement in both.

Corina Teodorescu, a fellow Romanian exchange student at USM, also became a good friend of Lavi's.[5] She shared how "Lavinia always made sure everybody completed their homework. 'Did you study, Corina? Did you do your homework?' I was more the socialite, but she was very serious and focused. You need to be focused and determined to reach the goals that Lavinia reached."

Teodorescu recalls how Lavi was "madly in love with Chris," and after she met Chris, he "would visit her at a USM learning center where she worked as an English and math tutor. Lavinia knew English so well that she was able to help American students with their writing, grammar and spelling."

Lavi's commitment to her education and love of learning were quickly recognized by Dr. Margaret Reimer,[6] a professor of English at the University of Southern Maine who also served as a mentor and trusted friend to her. Reimer recalls "Lavinia's remarkable reach" of English vocabulary and how her commitment to achieve complete fluency included "mastery of the idioms, subtleties and cultural nuances of the English language."

Over time, Lavi drew closer to Reimer. The mutual respect that can develop between a teacher who exudes a commitment to her profession and a serious student who genuinely wants to learn, no doubt, created a bond between the two.

Add to that dynamic the fact that Reimer had met Chris as a student in her freshman literature class and provided a safe, personal zone for Lavi to welcome her professor, not just as a teacher but as a friend. A woman she could trust and open up to, Lavi's comfort zone with her professor also built on the fact that Reimer's father had been a career Army officer who served in Vietnam. That significant part of Reimer's background made it all the more natural for her to relate to Lavinia with a credibility and perspective that comes with such a shared experience.

In my conversation with Reimer, she recalled Chris's "friendly, open-hearted personality, and earnest and conscientious approach to the course work." Among her memories is how he juggled his studies with the requirements of serving in the Maine Army National Guard. Among those memories is the occasion in which Chris delayed completing an assignment because of its direct conflict with his pending wedding to a "very special woman." When that very special woman became a student of Reimer's, she was quick to connect the dots.

Finding each other's half

To say Chris Gelineau's life was full during this period is an understatement. In addition to his academic studies, National Guard obligations, and continuing with another part-time pizza-delivery job, Chris took on a part-time job in 2001 with the USM maintenance crew. The unintended consequence of that decision brought him into the world of a young woman from Romania who was doing likewise.

While cleaning and painting college dorm rooms may not sound romantic, it often follows that the mundane of everyday life coincidentally connects two people. Good things can happen when you're not really looking, and according to Dimitrova, neither Lavi nor Chris were looking when they literally bumped their heads over a toilet seat while cleaning a bathroom in Portland Hall. Dimitrova recalls how "Lavi loved to tell the story as if it were the most romantic of all, love-story beginnings. Remembering that, always puts a smile on my face."

Given the memorable, head-bumping introduction and given Chris's technical wizardry skills, the next obvious step in the courtship was an offer to help Lavi with an alleged computer problem she was having. This was a good idea because Lavi was at first a bit skeptical to get involved with Chris, in part because of stereotypes of military men that caused her to be cautious. Perhaps her caution was influenced by the more rigid and domineering male culture in her native, postcommunist Romania or perhaps the caution was like that of many other women when they first meet a new guy, regardless of where he is from. More than likely a combination of all, but as Lavi got to know Chris, she found just the opposite—a sensitive, kind, and gentle man who shared her views of life and dreams of building a lasting life together.

If bumping heads over a toilet isn't destiny, what is? And to that point, Dimitrova remembers Lavi and Chris as "truly each other's halves," writing that "they were inseparable…and two of the few people in this world who were lucky to find *the One* who completes them."

"Chris was very logical, trustworthy, reliable. He had this cute baby face but was so incredibly mature. He was very calm in his interactions with others. I think of them as Lavi being fire and Chris being water, they balanced each other out. One thing that I feel was their couples' signature were the bright and wide smiles always on their faces! It was such a delight being around them. They were so attentive to everybody, so full of love and care for each other and for others."

Building on that memory, Dimitrova went on to describe Chris and Lavi as "great hosts, who would often organize parties, and I loved how the friends they invited had so much fun being together. It was always a very international company. My favorite part of all parties was when Lavinia would pick up the guitar and sing Romanian songs. There was this *Taganca* [Gypsy woman] song that I really liked and wanted to learn but never did." And not to be overlooked, "Chris would always make chocolate-chip cookies…and he was a master of those."

While they met in the spring of 2001, the horrific event of 9/11 was looming like a gathering hurricane. Tragically, only a handful were truly paying attention to the signs.

Within a short time of meeting, Chris and Lavi became engaged. In what might best be described as a sequel to how they met, Chris's proposal was a very unromantic but in its innocent spontaneity, uniquely romantic moment. While driving one day, he simply pulled over and popped the question. Smart move to pull over because no doubt, he reasoned that the question on his mind was a bit more significant than casually asking while driving.

Dimitrova described Chris's impromptu proposal, adding, "I know it seems a bit rushed for two people as thoughtful as they were to make such a huge step so soon after they had started dating but to me it made perfect sense…when you know, you know, and then there is only one thing to do—carpe diem [seize the day]!"

Within a year of their meeting, they were married on April 6, 2002, at the home of Chris's grandparents in Colchester, Vermont. It was a small wedding of mostly family on Chris's side and a few close friends, including Travis Scribner as best man and Dimitrova as maid of honor. Dimitrova remembers their wedding in Vermont as one of "happiest days of my life…they were my first really close friends to get married. I was beyond excited when they asked me to be their maid of honor…it was the most touching day of my life so far. I was so happy to see them at their happiest and to be able to share this amazing day with them. Chris's family absolutely loved Lavi, and it was obvious in their every word and gesture."

Reminiscing back to that special day, Dimitrova added a touching memory that speaks to the friendship and love that she shared with Lavi.

> Lavi was worried that she did not have enough money at the time to be the bride every little girl dreams to be. They wanted to have a second wedding in Romania for Lavi's family and friends. One March day we went to the Maine Mall to look for a wedding dress for Lavi.
>
> My father had given me several gift cards for Macy's. I offered to use them for a wedding dress. She wouldn't accept at first. Then I asked her to try the dresses she likes anyway. She did. I could see she liked one of them in particular, and told her I was using my gift cards to buy it for her. She still refused. I told her the gift cards were mine and I was to decide what I wanted to buy with them. She really liked the dress and knew I was not giving up so she surrendered. We bought the dress. Later, the two of us had such a great time trying hairstyles in my dorm room.

Romanian custom calls for two weddings: a civil ceremony to affirm the legal-government requirement and the second, a church wedding that recognizes the marriage within the desired religion of the couple.

With the ceremony in Colchester meeting the legal requirements, Lavi and Chris traveled to Romania a few weeks later to her hometown, Sibiu, for the church wedding. Attended primarily by Lavi's family and friends, the ceremony was held at the Orthodox Church in Sibiu. Interesting to note that in Romania, churches do not have a special, unique name but are recognized by the religious denomination and name of the street in which the church is located.

Thus, the Orthodox Church in Sibiu is identified as Orthodox Church on Stefan the Great Street (Strada Stefan cel Mare).

During the brief *honeymoon* period of their marriage, Lavi and Chris spent two weeks in Romania visiting with family and touring the country before heading back the 4,300-plus miles to Portland, Maine. That, of course, was the long path Lavi had traveled when her life ultimately intersected with the short, two-hundred-plus-mile path that Chris traveled from Bristol, Vermont, to Portland.

Back in Portland as newlyweds, Lavi and Chris settled into their home at the Princeton Apartments on Back Cove. Developed in the 1940s, the Princeton Apartments rest on slightly elevated land looking out on Portland's Baxter Boulevard.[7] Named after James Phinney Baxter who served as Portland's Mayor from 1893 to 1905, the boulevard is a gracefully designed semicircular road with a wide parallel walking-jogging path separating the apartment complex and fine homes from the 340-acre Back Cove tidal basin that leads out to Casco Bay and the Atlantic Ocean.

There is an irony of sorts as to where Chris and Lavi lived. Lining the boulevard are linden trees planted by the City of Portland on Memorial Day 1920 to honor the 1,073 Maine soldiers who died in Europe during World War I. The city chose Lindens because they were reminiscent of similar trees returning soldiers may have seen in France.[8]

The first tree was dedicated to Corporal Harold T. Andrews of Portland, the first Maine man to be killed in that war. Another tree was dedicated to Corporal Jacob Cousins, the first Jewish soldier from Portland to die. All branches of the military were recognized in the 1920 dedication of the boulevard, and in a nod to American ideals, Private Paolina Pellacia, an Italian immigrant and member of the Maine National Guard, was remembered for the sacrifice of his life in the *Battle of Belleau Wood*.

The monthlong fight of Belleau Wood took place in the northern French town of Chateau-Thiery and was the first major battle of the United States Army in WWI. The Allied victory was significant in responding to a major German offensive and is the source of the Maine National Guard motto, *To the Last Man*.

As a side bar, earlier in my career as assistant city manager of Portland, I had served as the lead staff to the city's bicentennial committee. One of the "visions" of the committee was to complete a pedestrian path as Baxter originally envisioned that would circumnavigate the tidal basin. The vision of the committee was realized in the early 2000s when significant infrastructure improvements along the I-295 corridor allowed for the widening of Tukey's Bridge, thereby accommodating the completion of the hike/bike trail.

Once home from their honeymoon, Lavi and Chris immersed themselves in the balancing act of full-time students and part-time jobs. For Chris, that included fulfilling his National Guard obligations. To the extent possible, they tried to share all three of their daily meals together.

Always the astute woman with an eye to the future, Lavi convinced Chris to retire from the pizza-delivery business and start building his résumé around his far more advanced skill set. His wife's sound advice quickly landed him with a position at Online Technologies. As an IT specialist, Chris put his knowledge and skills to work setting up networks and troubleshooting for client companies.

Lavi's encouragement, borne from her belief and love for her husband, complemented the commitment and trust they shared with each other. They were a true couple, each supporting and elevating the other, a critical guiding principle to a healthy, enduring, and loving relationship.

Background information regarding Lavinia and Chris Gelineau provided through email exchanges between the author and John Gelineau; the author with Vicky Chicoine; and author interviews with John and Iulia Gelineau in Sibiu, Romania, on April 13 through 18, 2018; and Vicky and Jesse Chicoine in Waterbury, Vermont, on June 30, 2018.

[1] Travis Scribner, "Remembering the Good Times," *Five Town News* (Bristol, Vermont, May 2004).

2. Franz Oberlerchner's email exchange with author on September 6, 2019.
3. Major Benjamin Leonard's interview through email exchanges with author on June 25, 2018.
4. This chapter includes extensive input through Denitiza Demitrova's email exchanges with the author during June, July, and August 2018.
5. Tess Nacelewicz (*Portland Press Herald* writer), *War Widow Eulogized as a 'Treasure'* (Mainetoday.com, April 10, 2005).
6. Margaret Reimer's interview with author in Bridgton, Maine, on August 15, 2018, and email exchanges.
7. Captain Jonathan D. Bratten, Maine Army National Guard, "World War I Memorial Trees along Portland's Baxter Boulevard," *Maine Historical Society, Maine Memory Network*.
8. Wikipedia, *City of Portland, Maine. Baxter Boulevard,* envisioned as one of four public parks surrounding the peninsula area (author's addition), designed by Olmstead, Olmstead & Eliot, 1895. The other three were Deering Oaks Park, Western Promenade, and Eastern Promenade.

April 6, 2002,
Colchester, Vermont

Wedding Day, Colchester, VT

Wedding Ceremony, Sibiu, Romania, May 18, 2002
Marriage laws in Romania require that a civil ceremony be held in a local city hall, in order to legally document the marriage. Usually, couples later have a formal church wedding and reception. Chris and Lavinia's, April 6, 2002 wedding in Vermont, fulfilled the legal requirements of their marriage. A ceremonial, church wedding was held on May 18, 2002, in Sibiu, Romania.

Honeyman, Sibiu, Romania

CHAPTER 4

September 11, 2001

It was another spectacular September day, a near-perfect repeat of the day at Peabody Pond. Instead of soaking in the sun and the peaceful tranquility of a classic Maine day in late summer, I was settling into my office at the Greater Portland Council of Governments in downtown Portland.[1]

While scrolling through email and reviewing the days schedule, a staff colleague, David Willauer, stopped by to share that his wife had just called with news that an airplane had flown in to the *World Trade Center.* My initial reaction would prove to be similar to that of many others who were just now hearing this news. I suggested to David that it must have been a small aircraft that somehow lost control or carelessly came too close to the building. No, he told me it was a much bigger plane. My mind was still in the world as we knew it, and so I reasoned that the cause was a mechanical problem, pilot error, or some combination.

It was a matter of just a few minutes before we came to learn what was taking place, and while huddled around a small TV, we witnessed in real time the shattering, unthinkable event of America under attack.

American Airlines Flight 11, traveling at 466 miles per hour and carrying ten thousand gallons of jet fuel, slammed into the North Tower of the World Trade Center at 8:46 a.m. And sixteen minutes later, with the whole world watching, United Airlines Flight 175, traveling at 590 miles per hour, hit the South Tower of the World Trade Center. This was soon followed by a third plane, American Airlines Flight 77, traveling at 530 miles per hour, as it crashed in to the western face of the Pentagon, triggering the collapse of a five-story section of the world's largest office building.[2]

At 9:45 a.m., with the realization that America was undergoing a carefully planned terrorist attack, the FAA ordered a complete shutdown of U.S. airspace and directed all aircraft to land at the nearest airport. International flights inbound were directed to our neighbors in Mexico and Canada. And in what would be the final hijacking, United Airlines Flight 93, traveling at 583 miles per hour, crashed in to a field, eighty miles southeast of Pittsburgh.

The 9/11 Commission would later express its opinion, but for the valiant efforts of its passengers in their attempt to regain control of the plane, the probable target of Flight 93 was either the U.S. Capitol or the White House.[3]

By late morning, both the North and South Towers had collapsed from the direct hits of the two Boeing 767s. And while 7 World Trade Center was not hit directly by either of the planes, the forty-seven-story building collapsed by late afternoon.

The magnitude and gravity of events was such that we had all drifted off and along with millions of others across the country, office doors quietly closed. People just wanted to be home. The mood of the city was eerily quiet as I left the office. Dead air tugged at my heart like the late afternoon stillness of November 22, 1963, a few short hours after President Kennedy was assassinated.

Whatever had seemed important at the beginning of the day was lost in the graphic, violent blur of death and destruction by the end of the day. But it was not the usual home-from-work routine. The mind-numbing events at ground zero would continue for days and months in a doomsday-like cycle of horror and destruction.

Nine eleven. For the generations who experienced that day, those two words are universally understood. We all know where we were and what we were doing. Having once participated in a meeting with engineering consultants and bankers at the famous North Tower restaurant, *Windows on the World*, I was haunted by the memory of the sheer height and vulnerability of that space. It was a feeling of utter suspension without a lifesaving constraint.

Many a night would pass before I stopped waking to the nightmare thought of those trapped in the planes or someone in the North Tower having a coffee only to look out to a giant commercial jet heading straight at them.

In the 101st to 105th floors of the North Tower, the "someone" were 658 employees of the financial services firm, Cantor Fitzgerald.[4] The firm's New York office had 960 employees at that time. Every single employee who was in the office that morning was killed, including Gary Lutnick, brother of Cantor Fitzgerald's CEO, Howard Lutnick, who was delayed arriving to the office because he had taken his son to his first day of kindergarten. A tragic, bittersweet reminder that each day is precious, and what begins as routine may suddenly be smothered in a life-changing event of profound and dramatic consequences.

Feelings of empathy, compassion, and concern for the innocent victims of violence and unexpected disasters is a natural response shared by all, except the most cold hearted. It's also entirely human to elevate that concern to a more personal, emotional level for people we love and know.

Imagine the Cantor Fitzgerald network of survivors and the same for the many generational families of the New York Fire and Police Departments and the other first responders. For those of us who were not personally touched, we do not *live with it* the same as they do. We remember, and we care and will never forget the horror. But every family directly impacted will always have that empty seat at the table and the penetrating pain of a loss that will never fully heal, such is the undefinable horror of that day.

In the years since 2001, the employees of Cantor Fitzgerald forgo 25 percent of salaries to donate to families who lost a loved one. Also, each year, the firm dedicates the money it takes in on a specific day, around $12 million after CEO Lutnick's contribution. Those funds go to charities and disaster recovery efforts.

During the day of 9/11, I thought of my sister, Marian, who was returning to her home in Alaska after a family visit in Maine.[5] I wondered how my cousin, Maine's first district congressman, Tom Allen, was doing in D.C., and whether my cousin Peter Allen, a pilot for Continental Airlines, was flying that day. Another cousin—there were eighteen of us—Christopher Allen, who has since passed away, caught an early morning flight from Logan to Atlanta and then on to Athens, Georgia, where he taught at the University of Georgia.

When Marian's bus arrived at Boston's Logan Airport, she recalls how the check-in process was routine and normal. At the boarding gate, though, there was confusion followed by an announcement that all outgoing flights were canceled. With the breaking news of the attacks on the World Trade Center, Logan completely shut down, thereby squashing Marian's itinerary that included a flight to New York City and from there, on to Seattle and Sitka, Alaska. She was one of the lucky ones who chose a later flight that morning for her flight back to the West Coast via New York. Marian would later tell me that on the return bus ride to Maine, she sat next to an American Airlines pilot who told her that he wasn't surprised, as they had been hearing rumors, "chatter," in recent months.

On September 11, 2001, Peter Allen was on a five-day break between flight assignments. Allen, who is now a captain for United Airlines, initially subscribed to the small-plane theory that so many of us did. Having logged many hours flying both the Boeing 767 and Boeing 757, Allen recalls "how it was all the more chilling to watch the second plane, knowing that it was being deliberately flown into the second tower." Surely, every pilot who commands such sophisticated aircraft and is entrusted with the awesome responsibility to safely deliver hundreds of passengers to their destinations saw themselves sitting in those cockpits.

At the time of the attacks, Congressman Allen was in a meeting with Leon Panetta, who at that time was the chair of the Pew Oceans Commission. In his book, *Dangerous Convictions,* Allen remembers the day as follows: "Shortly after 9 a.m. Leon was handed a note and told us that a plane [we all envisioned a small plane] had crashed into the World Trade Center."

Upon returning to his Longworth House office, Allen and his staff watched "in horror as another jetliner struck the second tower."

With the news that the Pentagon had been hit and the confirming evidence of the smoke that could be seen from their sixth-floor office windows, they left the building and headed to Allen's small apartment just a block away.

Maine's other congressman, Representative John Baldacci, was returning to his office from the congressional dining room where he had met up with a fellow colleague and friend, Representative Mike Doyle of Pennsylvania. The TVs in Baldacci's office was reporting that a small plane had flown into the World Trade Center, a report that was quickly revised to confirm that the small plane was actually a major commercial airline.

As Baldacci and his staff followed the events, he recalls thinking of it as a "modern day version of Pearl Harbor." Realizing that other planes were out there and the capitol was an obvious and clearly identifiable target, elevators were shut down and the capitol's architect and the Sergeant-at-Arms ordered evacuation by way of exiting on the back stairs.

Once outside and away from the building, the explosion and smoke from American Airlines Flight 77 crashing into the Pentagon could be heard and seen from the grounds of the capitol and felt underfoot from the massive blast. Reflecting on that day, Baldacci recalls a conversation a few days later with a security guard at the Pentagon. The guard described how earlier in the morning of 9/11, he had been standing outside at the point of impact only to watch a short time later as the AA jet zeroed in on its target, clipping utility poles on its descent in the final seconds. He shared with Baldacci how the fate of those moments "spiritually regenerated" him.

On 9/11, Kay Rand was serving as chief of staff to Maine's independent governor, Angus King, a role she would go on to fill when King was elected to the United States Senate in 2013. At the time of the attacks, King was meeting privately with Roxane Quimby in an effort to persuade her to drop the idea of creating a national park in northern Maine.

Unaware of what was taking place, King had made it clear that he did not want to be disturbed. With the details of the attacks confirming a terrorist plot, the governor's security detail became increasingly concerned that no one knew how far and wide the attack might be. With multiple state government issues and responsibilities requiring immediate attention, Rand intruded on the governor's meeting, urgently explaining, "We really need to go."

Leaving the state capitol, the governor and Rand traveled to the headquarters of the Maine National Guard for a hastily arranged meeting with the Maine National Guard command personnel and state legislative leaders. John W. "Bill" Libby, who at that time served as deputy adjutant general, recalls, "There was very little information at that time but an abundance of rumors and speculation… how wide was the conspiracy and possibility of further violence?" Of heightened concern to state officials was knowledge that two of the attackers had started their day with a flight from Portland to Boston.

One obvious decision for King was to close all government buildings and authorize all nonessential employees to go home. A small group of those attending the meeting, including King, decided to remain and bunk at the headquarters. During the night, the FBI arrived to brief King and the National Guard Command staff. As described by Libby, it became clear that the state was "ill equipped for dealing with a situation of this magnitude given its old decrepit building, small staff and then poor quality of its equipment."

King would later form a task force to address the significant organizational and operational shortcomings and weaknesses of the Maine National Guard. According to Libby, who in 2003 was appointed adjutant general of the Maine National Guard, "as more became known about the attacks and looming potential threats, the general consensus was that the Maine National Guard would be involved. The question, in what capacity, remained unanswered."

The consensus at the command level that the Maine National Guard would be involved in the response to the terrorist attack of 9/11 was shared by many of the soldiers and families of the Guard.

Best friends of Chris Gelineau from high school days in Vermont were Travis and Leslie Scribner. Travis had joined the Vermont Air National Guard while in high school and has continued to serve, rising to the rank of master sergeant with three deployments overseas. In thinking back to 9/11, Leslie remembers not only the horror of

9/11 but carries a bittersweet memory of a high school field trip to New York City and how Chris Gelineau snapped a photo of Travis and her kissing at the top of the World Trade Center. Over the years, that photo has taken on even deeper meaning and remains permanently in full view in their bedroom.

While Leslie cannot recall exactly how Chris and Lavinia responded to the 9/11 attacks, she remembers they all feared there would be war and Travis and Chris and would likely be deployed. At the time of 9/11, Chris's mother, Vicky Chicoine, shared that she never thought it would involve the National Guard.

Dr. Margaret Reimer learned of the attacks during her first semester teaching at the University of Southern Maine. Reimer who had both Chris and Lavinia as students was in between classes and like many who heard of the attacks from a secondary source, needed solid confirmation. Writing about that day, she described how "the large workspace near my office became hushed and everyone's faces were strained. The guys in the AV department down the hall invited us to watch the live video. We stood in stunned silence watching the smoke roll out of the roofs of the building and gasped as we began to see bodies plunging to the ground."

In Reimer's moving description of 9/11, she speaks to the work of her engineer father, who served in Vietnam and in the late 1960s, worked for the Army Corps of Engineers in Lower Manhattan. His building overlooked the construction site of the World Trade Center, providing what might be described as a time-lapse photo experience of its construction. Reimer recalled the many times her dad explained the remarkable and elaborate construction of the World Trade Center foundations. As the Twin Towers started to yield to the laws of physics and geometry, Reimer thought, *Surely my father was right and those buildings would survive… God, how I wish he had been correct.*

Upon arriving home, Reimer went for a walk. Years later, she wrote, "What struck me was how silent it was. I live outside town, but there is always noise from Rt 302 a mile away, and frequent sounds of airplanes, often up so high they are not visible but still can be heard. All that stopped. The only thing I could hear was birds. It was eerie and remained that way for a couple of weeks."

Any teacher, true to her or his profession, could not simply return to the programmed lesson plan right after 9/11 without opening a larger conversation. Dr. Margaret Reimer, professor of English at the University of Southern Maine, understood the significance of the moment and the mutually cathartic importance of open-classroom dialogue.

Reimer wrote:

> I had a profound sense that life had changed for good. When USM reopened, I took time in all my courses to talk with my students and to let them express their concerns. Chris Gelineau was my student that fall and was vocal about his sense that he needed to step up to defend his country. Most students were stunned, some really angry, and a few spent obsessive amount of time worrying about further dangers.

Captain Jonathan Batten, who is now the command historian of the Maine National Guard, was a fifteen-year-old high school student in Youngstown, Ohio. Describing 9/11 as the "first catastrophic event, seared into my consciousness," Batten likens it to the boomer generation awakening of a wider world when President Kennedy was murdered and the generation of his grandparents who were called to war following the December 7, 1941, Japanese attack on Pearl Harbor. Batten recalls how he watched "spellbound as the Twin Towers fell to the ground," adding that the terrorist attack motivated him to a career of service in the military. He combined that choice with his fascination for history, earning a bachelor and master's degree in history from the University of New Hampshire.

For Batten and others of his generation, 9/11 was a wake-up call of the truth that a much larger and complicated world awaited them. And like Batten, Maine National Guard public affairs officer,

Carl Lamb, was also in high school. On that day, he was in calculus class in Sanford, Maine.

Lieutenant Christopher Elgee was in his French class at the University of Maine when he heard of the attack. On returning to his dorm room, he followed the events and remembers feeling "an odd combination of being overwhelmed and numb at the same time." Three months later, he was commissioned as an officer, and his "feelings shifted from shock to resolve," resulting in volunteering to mobilize with the 133rd. Elgee continues to serve in the Maine National Guard, holding the rank of lieutenant colonel.

On 9/11, Franz Oberlerchner heard of the attack while standing at the top of the Victory Tower at Fort Jackson in Columbia, South Carolina. Having joined the National Guard in his senior year of high school in 2000, Oberlerchner was completing his basic training requirement, which included climbing and repelling skills on the forty-foot Victory Tower. It wasn't until later that night that he saw the footage of the planes crashing into the towers. Being told the next day by a high-ranking general that the attacks would eventually bring them all to "foreign lands…was like getting an ice-cold bucket of water being dumped over my head from a solid sleep."

After six years in the Navy, including fifty-four months of submarine duty, Lieutenant Todd Crawford of the Maine Army National Guard—attorney in his civilian world—was at Portland District Court doing "lawyer stuff" and noticed on his pager that his wife had been trying to reach him. He returned the call from the courthouse using a pay phone and learned of the attacks. Crawford was "stunned" with the news and understood "instantly" that September 11, 2001, would have "consequences for him personally."

Without any directive, formal or otherwise, Crawford's years in the military compelled him to essentially "report for duty" and drive to the 133rd Engineering Battalion at the Maine National Guard Armory in Portland. According to Crawford, others in the battalion reacted in the same spontaneous way, and together, they joined the millions who were glued to the news, speculating as to the *who, why, and what* would happen next. But unlike the vast majority of their fellow citizens, the members of the National Guard are ever mindful of the military side of their life and its linkage to the solemn oath they take to defend and protect the United States of America against all enemies, both foreign and domestic. For Crawford, 9/11 began the emotional and life-changing transition to be ready for active-duty deployment.

Like Todd Crawford, Adam Cote is now a practicing Maine attorney. On a personal note, my meeting with Cote was very much a déjà vu moment. His law firm had not only taken over the offices that the Greater Portland Council of Governments had occupied for a number of years prior to moving to their present location, but Cote was occupying the very same office that I once sat in. Not that we needed an icebreaker, but to leave it unsaid would have been weird. Coincidentally, too, the offices were where Lavinia had worked during her internship and where I had met Chris Gelineau.

On 9/11, Cote and his wife were on a long-planned trip to Europe, traveling by rail from Seville to Toledo, Spain. He recalls how "all the folks on the train were on their phones talking about what happened," and with his Columbian-born wife, fluent in Spanish, they quickly learned what had happened. Over the next couple of days, they remained in Toledo, watching the extensive twenty-four seven coverage of the attacks on TV. In a journal of the trip that he was keeping, Cote wrote that he believed Osama bin Laden as "the most likely culprit" and further opined that "I would be going to war sometime soon."

At that time, Cote had two more years on his National Guard enlistment contract and was thinking of getting out. Over the immediate days following the attacks, he and his wife spent many hours walking and exploring Toledo and discussing their future. Rather than leaving the military at this time, Cote explained to his wife that he wanted "to pursue a commission as an officer because if I was going to deploy again, I wanted to have responsibilities… I was able to convince her for me to pursue that, which I did." When the 133rd deployed to Iraq in 2004, Lieutenant Cote was selected as a platoon leader of Bravo Company.

Greg Madore, who retired from the National Guard in 2006 as a master sergeant, was working at Fairchild Semiconductor in

South Portland. When the second tower crumbled to the ground, a coworker nudged him as they watched the scene on TV, predicting that "you're going to be going overseas." Almost instantly, his pager went off with "a note to call into operations at Camp Keyes to help someone set up and test satellite phones."

Alicia Newbegin, who worked full time for the Maine Army Reserve National Guard, explained that "At the time of the attacks, I was in my office at the Stevens Avenue Armory in Portland. One of the recruiters came down and told me so we all went to the break room to watch it on TV. I just stood, and tears welled up, and thought, *Oh my gosh*, and then the phone started ringing. I was in a daze the rest of the day."

Staff Sergeant Hal Fitch joined the Maine National Guard in 1987 after serving three years in the regular Army. He was well aware of the possibility of deployment having been around when his unit of the Maine National Guard was placed on alert status during the 1991 Desert Storm initiative. On 9/11, Fitch was working for a consulting firm in Pittsfield, Maine. As Fitch watched the horror of the attacks unfold that morning, he "instinctively knew we were going to war."

Lieutenant Colonel John Jansen, who would go on to serve as the battalion commander of the 133rd Engineering Battalion during its deployment to Iraq, was working at the battalion's operations Center in Augusta. After the second strike on the other tower, "we realized we were witnessing a terrorist act." Within a short period, "we started seeing heavy message traffic from the National Guard Headquarters regarding the incidents and security measures that we needed to put in place."

While he assumed there would be some retaliation when responsibility for the attacks was established, Jansen wrote in an email, "I had no idea of the magnitude of response and the sequence of events that would trigger. I did not imagine at that time that we would soon be deploying troops to include Maine soldiers to Afghanistan and going to Iraq was not something I had remotely considered."

Congress and the president come together

Early that evening, America's representatives to Congress convened on the steps of the U.S. Capitol, and after brief remarks from Republican House Speaker Dennis Hestert and Senate Majority Leader Tom Daschle, Democrat, the gathered Republicans and Democrats broke out into a spontaneous singing of *God Bless America*. Remembering that moment on the tenth anniversary of 9/11, Maine Senator Olympia Snowe said, "We sang to send a message to the country and the world that freedom would never be crushed by the blunt and remorseless instrument of terror." Every once in a while, the true ties that bind us serve to remind us of how much we share, thereby begging the question: Why can't those brief moments be more than brief moments?

Speaking from the Oval Office to the nation, shortly after the congressional gathering, President George W. Bush said, "A great people has been moved to defend a great nation. Terrorist attacks can shake the foundations of our biggest buildings, but they cannot touch the foundation of America. These acts shatter steel, but they cannot dent the steel of American resolve."[6]

The president, who had learned of the attacks while reading to a kindergarten class in Florida, praised the heroic efforts of the first responders who we later learned had played a critical role in the evacuation of hundreds if not thousands of workers from the Twin Towers. And it would later be confirmed that of the 415 emergency workers who lost their lives, 85 percent were firefighters, with the balance being NYPD, Port Authority Police, and Paramedics.[7]

Concluding his brief remarks with a call for unity "in our resolve for justice and peace," Bush reminded the world that "America has stood down enemies before, and we will do so this time. None of us will ever forget this day, yet we go forward to defend freedom and all that is good and just in our world."

It was not just an attack on America but an attack on the *idea* of America, grounded as we are on the real and aspirational ideals that combine to form a country of immigrants, unique in the history of human existence. America's diversity and strength was illuminated by the horrific death count that included citizens of other nations, cultures, and religions. Of the 2,976 killed on the day of the attack, 372 were non-US citizens from 115 different countries.[8]

As horrific as it was, consider that fifty thousand people were employed in businesses housed at the World Trade Center with a daily average of up to two hundred thousand visitors. If the attacks had occurred later in the morning, the numbers murdered and injured would have been even more staggering. Transfixed in what we all knew would be a defining and memorializing date in history, the country was numb with shock, emotion, and grief. The massive impact of the attacks with haunting scenes of people jumping from the towers; first responders entering the burning, smoke-filled buildings and never returning; and survivors engulfed in choking dust and debris, running from the buildings, running from the scene, trying to find safety somewhere, anywhere.

Each day brought new gruesome details of the attacks with heart-wrenching stories of those who died and the heroism of first responders. There was constant conjecture of how it happened, who was involved along with the speculation of what America's response should be. All these issues got played and replayed along with the footage that no matter how many times I saw it, the brutality and horror defied words.

It was all the more chilling to learn that Mohammed Atta, the leader of the nineteen terrorists who carried out the attacks along with Abdulaziz Alomari, had spent the night of September 10 at a motel in the shadows of South Portland's sprawling Maine Mall complex. With the exception of thirty-three-year-old Atta, all the other hijackers were in their twenties at the time of 9/11.[9] Tragically misguided and twisted with a premeditated intent to kill, the terrorist hijackers came of age to a much larger and complicated world.

Motivated by Osama bin Laden, a cultlike, anti-Semitic leader, they focused hate, bias, and violence against those who held beliefs and a culture contrary to theirs. That underlying contempt has framed much of history throughout the centuries. Sometimes the violence is the work of many and sometimes the work of one, as seen in the 1993 bombing of a federal office building in Oklahoma City. Carried out by twenty-seven-year-old Timothy McVeigh, a decorated veteran of the Gulf War, McVeigh's act of domestic terrorism killed 168 men, women, and children.[10]

Tough to contemplate the thought process of Atta and his band of obsessed bin Laden followers as they prepared for their rendezvous in Boston the next day. As the first ray of sun touched the Maine coast, Atta and Alomari were boarding U.S. Air Flight 5930 at the Portland International Jetport for the short flight to Boston's Logan Airport.[11] By nightfall, their terrorist conspiracy would rock the globe with a Richter scale magnitude, triggering after shock tremors that two decades later continue to pierce the political, social, and economic order of planet Earth.

On September 20, 2001, nine days after the attacks, President Bush addressed a joint session of Congress.[12] Having visited ground zero just three days after the attacks, the president called on themes of history and courage, citing the remarkable efforts of passengers on United Airlines Flight 93 that prevented additional death and destruction on the ground and "the endurance of rescuers, working past exhaustion…the unfurling of flags, the lighting of candles, the giving of blood, and the saying of prayers…in English, Hebrew, and Arabic."

At this fragile moment, George W. Bush understood the heavy responsibility of serving as president of the United States requires a commitment to represent all the people and to do so through setting a tone befitting of America's ideals. He expressed concern that with emotions running at fever pitch, the knee-jerk response of some would be to profile all Muslims as the enemies of America.

Three days before his speech to Congress and to underscore that commitment to the ideals of America, Bush visited the *Islamic Center* of Washington where he met with followers of Islam for what he described as "wide-ranging discussions on the matter at hand." Speaking to those present, which included the national media, he went on to say, "The face of terror is not the true faith of Islam. That's not what Islam is all about. Islam is peace. These terrorists don't represent peace. They represent evil and war. When we think of Islam we think of a faith that brings comfort to a billion people around the world… America counts millions of Muslims amongst our citizens, and Muslims make an incredibly valuable contribution to our country."[13]

To add further emphasis on the importance of maintaining unity and respect for all faiths, Bush said, "I want to speak directly to Muslims throughout the world. We respect your faith. It's practiced freely by many millions of Americans, and by millions more in countries that America counts as friends. Its teachings are good and peaceful." In doing so, he called out the terrorists, declaring that they are "traitors to their own faith."

Bush's consistent message of using the power of the presidency to set a respectful tone of tolerance and appreciation for Islam may well have averted an ugly political and societal response that would only make matters worse. His leadership on this issue was recognized eleven years later by Samuel G. Freedman of the *New York Times*.

In a September 7, 2012, piece, "Six Days After 9/11, Another Anniversary Worth Honoring," Freedman commended Bush for speaking out against harassment of Arabs and Muslims in the immediate aftermath of the terrorist attacks.[14]

In his September 20 speech to Congress, Bush shared to the world that "the evidence we have gathered all points to a collection of loosely affiliated terrorist organizations known as al-Qaeda and how they were behind the bombing of the USS Cole and US embassies in Tanzania and Kenya." He named Osama bin Laden as al-Qaeda's leader and described how they recruit worldwide and manage terrorist training camps in Afghanistan, a country that was largely controlled but not legally governed (at that time) by the Taliban regime.

Of note, by the mid to late 1990s, the Taliban had taken control of much of Afghanistan in order to advance their strict Muslim code of behavior. In the Pashto language that is spoken by many Afghans, the word Taliban means "students," and unlike the millions of Muslims who practice a peaceful interpretation of their faith, the Taliban followers espouse an extreme view that supports—and in fact, celebrates—violence or whatever means may be necessary to achieve their goal of universal purity.[15]

In citing the Taliban as "aiding and abetting" al-Qaeda, Bush made a number of demands, including the closing of their training camps and handing over of all terrorists and those who play a supporting role. He warned that "These demands are not open to negotiation or discussion. The Taliban must act, and act immediately. They hand over the terrorists, or they will share in their fate."

In his warning to the Taliban, President Bush put the world on notice that "From this day forward, any nation that continues to harbor or support terrorism will be regarded by the United States as a hostile regime." He cautioned that "Americans should not expect one battle, but a lengthy campaign, unlike any other we have ever seen" and to help fully coordinate the local, state, and national effort, the president announced the creation of a new Cabinet-level agency, the *Office of Homeland Security.*

Of relevance to the story of Chris and Lavi and the many others with military obligations, Bush concluded his remarks to the Congress with a challenge for America's military "to be prepared… many will be involved in this effort, from FBI agents to intelligence operatives to the reservists we have called to active duty."

---

[1] Established in 1969, *The Greater Portland Council of Governments* provides land use, energy, transportation, and economic development services to its member municipalities, Cumberland County Government, and other public service providers.
[2] www.britannica.com, *September 11 attacks / History, Summary, Location, Time Line* (September 7, 2022).
[3] *The 9/11 Commission Report: Final Report of the National Commission on Terrorist Attacks Upon the United States* (July 22, 2004).
[4] Max Reyes, "Cantor Fitzgerald's 9/11 Tragedy, We Lost Them All" (www.bloomberg.com, updated on September 10, 2021).

5. Beginning with "*During that day, I thought of my sister,*" all eighteen interviews in that section, "*Where were you, and what were you doing on 9/11?*" were conducted by the author directly or via phone or email.
6. George W. Bush, *9/11 Address to the Nation* (delivered on September 11, 2001, at the Oval Office).
7. "September 11 by Numbers," *New York Magazine* (updated 2021).
8. Britannica Online Encyclopedia, *Osama bin Laden*.
9. Wikipedia, *Hijackers in the September 11 Attacks*.
10. Timothy McVeigh, www.fbi.gov.oklahomacitybombing.
11. Sean Murphy, In Maine, an unanswered question remains about the events on 9/11 (specctrumlocalnews.com, September 9, 2021).
12. George W. Bush, *Address to Joint Session of Congress Following 9/11 Attacks* (delivered on September 20, 2001).
13. George W. Bush, *Islam is Peace*, remarks at the Islamic Center of Washington, D.C. (September 17, 2001).
14. Samuel G. Freedman, "Six Days After 9/11, Another Anniversary Worth Honoring," *New York Times* (September 7, 2012).
15. Britannica, bin Laden, *Building al-Qaeda*.

CHAPTER 5

Afghanistan: Operation Enduring Freedom

AFTER NEARLY THREE WEEKS, IT WAS OBVIOUS that the Taliban was not going to meet the demands that President Bush had outlined in his speech to Congress on September 20, foremost of which was to "deliver to United States authorities all leaders of al-Qaeda who hide in your land."

In response to the Taliban's refusal to comply, on October 7, Bush went on national TV to announce that "on my orders, United States military strikes against al-Qaeda terrorist training camps and military installations of the Taliban regime in Afghanistan have begun."[1] Speaking from the Treaty Room in the White House, Bush outlined the operational support from Great Britain, Canada, France, Australia, and Germany.

In addition to outlining the objectives of the military initiative, President Bush noted that in parallel with military operations, food, medicine, and other supplies were to be air-dropped to the people of Afghanistan. And consistent with all his previous public remarks during this period, Bush reiterated that "we are the friends of almost a billion worldwide who practice the Islamic faith." He added the caveat that "the United States of America is an enemy of those who aid terrorists and of the barbaric criminals who profane a great religion by committing murder in its name." And he warned that "every nation has a choice to make."

In announcing the launch of *Operation Enduring Freedom* (OEF), Bush cautioned that "today we focus on Afghanistan, but the battle is broader," and to meet the challenges going forward, he sought to reassure Americans of the initiatives that were being taken to strengthen the country's security, citing the stepped-up efforts in law enforcement and intelligence gathering.

Building on his earlier reference to the National Guard, Bush announced, "At my request, many governors have activated the National Guard to strengthen airport security. We have called up reserves to reinforce our military capability and strengthen the protection of our homeland."

Angus King of Maine was one of those governors, and in the immediate days following 9/11, some elements of the Maine National Guard (MENG) were used to strengthen security at Maine's airports and assist with border security along the United States–Canadian border.[2] Because the initial military effort of OEF was to carry out a dominating air assault within Afghanistan, the Maine Air National Guard was among the National Guard units to be deployed by United States Central Command (CENTCOM) for logistical support in the war on terrorism. CENTCOM's mission was to disrupt and destroy al-Qaeda terror training bases and operations in Afghanistan.

The U.S. led air strikes in Afghanistan that Bush had announced on October 7 targeted Taliban-controlled infrastructure and the training bases that formed the backbone of al-Qaeda. Over the ensuing two months, the combination of air power, together with U.S. Special Operations Forces and the anti-Taliban Northern Alliance of Afghan were successful in rooting out many al-Qaeda and Taliban leaders. Their combined efforts resulted in the capture of the city of Mazar-i-Sharif and its strategically important airport. By mid-November, the Taliban had lost its control of Kabul, the Afghan capital, and the northern city of Kandahar and the caves of Tora Bora.[3]

The military response to the 9/11 attacks was received favorably throughout much of world. Bush was effective in securing the sympathy and good will of world leaders, most of the countries of the

Middle East, NATO, and Asian allies. The restraint that his father had applied a decade earlier during the Gulf War was undoubtedly reassuring to many and reinforced by the rapid and relatively successful removal of the Taliban from its grip on Afghanistan.

With the Taliban's loss of control of Afghanistan, President Bush declared in his first *State of the Union*[4] address on January 29, 2002 that "the American flag flies over our embassy in Kabul. Terrorists who once occupied Afghanistan now occupy cells at Guantanamo Bay." To a rousing ovation, Bush declared that "America and Afghanistan are now allies against terror. We will be partners in rebuilding that country and this evening we welcome the distinguished interim leader of a liberated Afghanistan: Chairman Hamid Karzai."

Bush took the occasion of the *State of the Union* to roll out a sweeping global review of terrorism, specifically citing North Korea, Iran, and Iraq as an "axis of evil" that in combination with their "terrorist allies," threaten "the peace of the world."

The president's most pointed words were directed at Iraq, thereby setting the stage for the mission that would become known as *Operation Iraqi Freedom* (OIF). "Iraq continues to flaunt its hostility toward America and to support terror. The Iraqi regime has plotted to develop anthrax and nerve gas and nuclear weapons for over a decade. This is a regime that has already used poison gas to murder thousands of its own citizens, leaving bodies of mothers huddled over their dead children. This is a regime that agreed to international inspections then kicked out the inspectors. This is a regime that has something to hide from the civilized world."

Bush's shot over the bow warning of "a lengthy campaign, unlike any other we have ever seen," set the table for a far wider military response than just Afghanistan. Viewed in that context, the environmental-geographic challenges facing Operation Enduring Freedom and Operation Iraqi Freedom were daunting.

Assuming that I am typical of most Americans who have never set foot in Afghanistan or Iraq, I have no direct appreciation for the size of the region and the countries within.

At the time of the *State of the Union* speech, the initial mission in Afghanistan—i.e., taking out the Taliban-controlled terrorist training camps and as many of its leaders as possible—had been effective. Going forward, though, the physical challenges of successfully holding the balance of power while transforming the country were daunting, given the imposing, mile-high mountains that frame its predominantly rural population of forty million people. Close to 50 percent of the total land area of Afghanistan is above 6,560 feet. And the country covers an area of just under 250,000 square miles, making it comparable to the 269,000 square miles of Texas.[5]

Iraq's 168,000 square miles make it slightly larger than California's 164,000 square miles, and its population of forty-one million exceeds California's by two million. Afghanistan and Iraq, together with Iran, Saudi Arabia, Kuwait, Jordan, Syria, and Turkey have an estimated population of 265 million people with a combined area of about 2.7 million square miles, or slightly less than the size of Australia.[6]

Factor in brutal heat, disproportionate cold, harsh mountain terrain, and blinding sandstorms, no wonder the extra caution voiced by military leaders in fighting a potentially long, protracted war under such conditions. Physical barriers are challenging enough, but the probability of "success" is made all the more challenging given the extreme social, cultural, and political differences between the Middle East and Western Bloc nations.

At the time of the 9/11 attacks, Richard Clarke was serving as the national coordinator for security, infrastructure protection, and counterterrorism. Clarke was first appointed to that position by President Clinton and reappointed by President Bush. Over his three decades of government service, Clarke held high-level positions under four presidents and over that period, grew to be recognized as a foremost authority on global and domestic terrorism. In particular, he developed an in-depth knowledge of al-Qaeda under the leadership of Osama bin Laden.[7]

Unlike millions of peaceful followers of Islam, Osama bin Laden developed an extreme militant view of Islam, believing that all Muslims should carry out a *jihad* or holy war, with the goal to create a pure Islamic state. Thus, bin Laden considered the Soviet invasion of Afghanistan in the 1980s as a war against Islam and traveled to

Afghanistan to meet with the insurgent leaders. His efforts included fundraising and recruitment of volunteers to join the jihad.[8]

During this period, bin Laden remained primarily in Afghanistan and Pakistan. Smart and physically tall, a feature that one day would help identify his whereabouts and death, in 1988, bin Laden created a computer database of the volunteers who were part of the Afghan resistance.[9]

It wasn't until 1996 that the bin Laden network was understood by Western sources to be organized under the name *al-Qaeda*, which in Arabic means "the base." In *Against All Enemies*, Clarke wrote, "The network also had a name: the foundation or base, as in the foundation of a building. Osama bin Laden, son of a building contractor, had called his terrorist network by an Arabic word, al-Qaeda. It was the first piece, the necessary base for the edifice that would be a global theocracy, the great Caliphate."[10]

After the collapse of the Soviet Union, bin Laden returned to Saudi Arabia to a triumphant welcome. The aura of good feelings was brief when the Saudi government would not approve bin Laden's request to use al-Qaeda fighters instead of the U.S. military in the event of an invasion by Saddam Hussein's Iraqi Army.

As the al-Qaeda-inspired attacks increased, the Saudi government stripped bin Laden of his citizenship and his assets. With the welcome mat yanked from under him, bin Laden left Saudi Arabia and moved to Sudan in 1991. From there, he focused on carrying out maximum force against the growing American presence in the Muslim world and also spent time in Yemen organizing and training Islamic militants to carry the jihad around the world.

In the eight-month period between Bush assuming the presidency and the terrorist attacks on America, Clarke had been warning the White House of the growing threat of a major terrorist attack with high probability that it would be organized and executed by al-Qaeda. Not until the fateful day of September 11, 2001, was Clarke provided the opportunity to meet directly with Bush.[11]

In his book *Against All Enemies,* Clarke writes that on returning to the White House (on September 12), "I expected to go back to a round of meetings examining what the next attacks could be, what our vulnerabilities were, what we could do about them in the short term. Instead, I walked into a series of discussions about Iraq. At first I was incredulous that we were talking about something other than getting al-Qaeda. Then I realized with almost a sharp physical pain that Rumsfeld and Wolfowitz were going to try to take advantage of this national tragedy to promote their agenda about Iraq. Since the beginning of the administration, indeed well before, they had been pressing for a war with Iraq. My friends in the Pentagon had been telling me that the word was we would be invading Iraq sometime in 2002."[12]

In *The 9/11 Commission Report*, there is an exchange between President Bush and British Prime Minister Tony Blair during their meeting on September 20, 2002. Blair asks about Iraq, and "the President replied that Iraq was not the immediate problem. Some members of his administration, he commented, 'had expressed a different view, but he was the one responsible for making decisions.'"[13]

Richard Clarke had a different view from Paul Wolfowitz, Donald Rumsfeld, and others. On the day of the Bush-Blair meeting, Clarke had submitted a memorandum to National Security Advisor Condoleezza Rice as requested by Bush. Clarke's findings included that there is "no compelling case that Iraq had either planned or perpetrated the attacks."[14]

Clarke's was not the only voice trying to get the attention of the president and others on the menace posed by al-Qaeda. Secretary of State Colin Powell felt likewise, as did CIA Director George Tenet, who met regularly with Bush on the issues of national security.

In Clarke's update of his book, he writes in the *Forward* "that George Tenet's daily briefings for the President mentioned al-Qaeda on forty occasions, often with great urgency, prior to 9/11." Clarke goes on to write that as outlined in his book and "as the *9/11 Commission Report* makes painfully clear, the President did little else about terrorism prior to September 11 despite the alarm bells from George Tenet."[15]

Shortly after Bush's inauguration in January 2001, Clarke had been trying to get a meeting of the *principal's committee* of high-level Cabinet types to discuss the threat of al-Qaeda. In its final report,

The 9/11 Commission wrote, "On the day of the meeting [September 4, 2001], Clarke sent Rice an impassioned personal note that was critical of U.S. counterterrorism efforts past and present.

"Clarke's message asserted that the 'real question' before the principals, 'are we serious about dealing with the al-Qaeda threat?… Is al-Qaeda a big deal?… Decision makers should imagine themselves on a future day when the CSG [the interagency Counterterrorism Security Group] has not succeeded in stopping al Qaeda attacks and hundreds of Americans lay dead in several countries, including the US,… What would those decision makers wish that they had done earlier? That future day could happen at any time." Clarke wrote that just one week *before* the September 11 attacks.[16]

---

[1] George W. Bush, *Afghanistan Address to the Nation: Operation Enduring Freedom* (delivered on October 7, 2001).
[2] Wikipedia, *Maine Air National Guard, History*: "After 9/11, elements of every Maine Air National Guard unit were activated in support of the Global War on Terrorism."
[3] U.S. Department of State archive, *The Global War on Terrorism: The First 100 Days* (information released online from January 20, 2001 to January 20, 2009).
[4] George W. Bush, *2002 State of the Union Address* (January 29, 2002).
[5] Wikipedia, *Geography of Afghanistan*.
[6] Wikipedia, *Geography of Iraq*.
[7] Richard A. Clarke, *Against All Enemies: Inside America's War on Terror*.
[8] Ibid.
[9] Britannica Online, *Osama bin Laden*.
[10] Ibid. *Osama bin Laden, Building al-Qaeda*.
[11] Clarke, *Against All Enemies*, 148.
[12] Ibid. 30.
[13] *The 911 Commission Report*, 336.
[14] Ibid. 334
[15] Clarke, *Against All Enemies: Forward to the Paperback Edition* xxxiii.
[16] Clarke, *Note to Rice*, 301.

Chapter 6

Operation Iraqi Freedom What Are We Doing?

No sooner had Afghanistan been brought under a semblance of control than the nation-building initiative of *Operation Iraqi Freedom* went into high gear. At that time, I remember thinking, *Why are we loosening our grip on Afghanistan so soon, a nation of warlords, a breeding ground for terrorist expansion, inhumane treatment of women, extreme poverty, and dysfunctional government?*

Rather than enabling the legacy of conflict to continue, why not help with a focus on securing the peace and building a stable, community-oriented government whose mission is to get the things done that people need? Put the ideology battles aside. The universal needs of any society are safety, housing, food, water, medical access, and education. Success is a more likely outcome—both short and long term—when a local labor force is built around such goals.

These were the goals that one would think President Bush was referring to in his speech to the cadets at the Virginia Military Institute in April of 2002. Specifically, he advocated for a "Marshall Plan" type response to help rebuild Afghanistan.[1] Not to speculate too far from that moment, but if we had truly committed to a community building partnership with Afghanistan, would the last two decades have ended as they did?

The sudden shift to reduce our presence in Afghanistan and put a bull's-eye on Iraq hardly seemed to be a formula for rebuilding, particularly when the first order of governance must be to ensure the safety and security of its people. This is priority number one that my good friend, Ambassador Rick Barton, has repeatedly made throughout his decades of service in some of the most war-torn, dangerous regions of the world.

In *Peace Works: America's Unifying Role in a Turbulent World*, Barton writes, "As long as people are being shot, physically intimidated, and starving, do not expect progress in other areas. Once conditions are safe, building trust and pluralistic self-governance will foster opportunities in a peaceful, democratic environment."[2]

The attack on Afghanistan coming as it did within a month of 9/11 was driven by a president who clearly understood that the American public, myself included, and Congress wanted and expected an appropriate response and they were looking to their president to deliver on that expectation.

Those feelings were buttressed with strong global and media support of the objective to hunt down Osama bin Laden and remove the Taliban from its control of Afghanistan. I feel safe in saying that what the American public did not want was a two-decade conflict that brought the chaos full circle, ironically leaving Afghanistan officially back in the hands of the Taliban. Talk about the dog chasing its tail. Like Vietnam, Afghanistan was a tragic event in world and American history. For blame-game purposes, there is plenty of evidence that both Republican and Democratic politicians contributed mightily to that outcome.

Operation Enduring Freedom offered a situational time frame that lent itself to swift and decisive presidential action, framed as it was by the dramatic and definable event of 9/11. At its core, the immediate mission of OEF was to root out the Taliban-supported al-Qaeda recruitment and training cells and with any luck, bin Laden himself.

By contrast, *Operation Iraqi Freedom* was a much larger and complicated initiative and would take time to fully execute. The details of a serious and comprehensive planning for military operations and post-military governance would require a commitment to a process that seeks objective input from a range of congressional, political, and military sources together with the outside expertise needed to meet the postwar needs of rebuilding communities and creating viable economies.

Ostensibly, the military effort in Iraq was to secure the peace for its citizens in order to promote a more stable world order. That is as it should be. The vision, though, was a more ideologically based, nation-building objective driven by an assumption that the transition to a democracy would be relatively easy.

The Bush administration's *Operation Iraqi Freedom* team evolved as a small and powerful group whose minds and ideologies were set on invading Iraq and doing so preemptively. Seizing on the events of 9/11, they saw the opportunity to remove Saddam Hussein from power and move forward with their nation-building vision for Iraq.

Consisting of Vice President Cheney and Defense Secretary Rumsfeld, the team formed a tight strategy-and-planning inner circle that included ideologues, Deputy Defense Secretary Paul Wolfowitz, Richard Pearle of the Defense Policy Board, Scooter Libby (the vice president's chief of staff) together with Douglas Feith (the Defense Department undersecretary for policy), and Condoleezza Rice (the national security advisor to the president).

As described by Richard Clarke in the previous chapter, within a few hours after the 9/11 attack on America, there was talk of attack on Iraq. Clarke further amplified that reaction with the following passage in his book, *Against All Enemies*.

"By the afternoon on Wednesday [September 13], Secretary Rumsfeld was talking about broadening the objectives of our response and 'getting Iraq.' Secretary Powell pushed back, urging focus on al-Qaeda. Relieved to have some support, I thanked Colin Powell and his deputy, Rich Armitage. I vented, 'Having been attacked by al Qaeda, for us to now go bombing Iraq in response would be like our invading Mexico after the Japanese attacked us at Pearl Harbor.'"[3]

The nation-building objective was confirmed by President Bush at a news conference on July 8, 2002. Regarding the issue of Iraq, Bush said, "It's a stated policy of this government to have a regime change. And it hasn't changed. And we'll use all the tools at our disposal to do so."[4]

As the likelihood of war grew, Secretary of State Powell met with President Bush on August 5, 2002, at the White House. "You are going to be the proud owner of twenty-five million people," Powell said. "You will own all their hopes, aspirations, and problems... It's going to suck the oxygen out of everything... This will be your first term."[5]

Contrary to Powell's concerns and to the fact that WMD had not yet been confirmed, Vice President Cheney declared in a speech to the Veterans of Foreign Wars on August 26, 2002, that "There is no doubt that Iraq has weapons of mass destruction." He went on to say, "We realize that wars are never won on the defensive. We must take the battle to the enemy." He further declared, "Time is not on our side... The risks of inaction are far greater than the risks of action."[6] Cheney's categorical "no-doubt" insistence without the evidence further confirms that the policy decision was war and we'll deal with the consequences after we win the battle.

Retired Marine Corps General Anthony Zinni was at that VFW event and would later assert that "In my time at CENTCOM, I watched the intelligence and never—not once—did it say, 'He has WMD.'" After his retirement, Zinni continued to hold top-secret clearance, and in his consultant work for the CIA, he was able to say that "it was never there, never there." Zinni would go on to make public his doubts, saying of Saddam Hussein, "I'm not convinced we need to do this now... I believe he is...containable at this moment."[7]

Similar caution was shared by another retired four-star general, Norman Schwarzkopf, who had gained fame during the Gulf War. Like many in the Army, Schwarzkopf thought that "Rumsfeld, Wolfowitz, Feith, and their subordinates lacked the experience or knowledge to make sound military judgments by themselves and were ignoring the better informed advice of senior generals."[8]

Congressional resolution

There is no debating that Saddam Hussein was a brutal, cruel dictator. However, he was the president of a sovereign nation and like all dictators, would not politely leave if requested.

There were two potential paths for Hussein's removal: (1) commit to continue a policy of containment, freezing of assets, and the search for WMD and (2) invade Iraq, remove Hussein from power, and continue to search for WMD. The decision of the Bush administration appeared to conclude that rather than mark time waiting for confirmation of WMD, move forward in parallel with the military option. If WMD are confirmed, all the better.

Given the circumstance of a planned attack on a sovereign nation, the formal involvement of Congress would be legally and politically advisable. And as confident that the Bush team was in the outcome of a military strike, there were steps to be taken and military plans to be developed.

For many years, conventional thinking assumed, but for the constitutional checks and balances establishing civilian control of America's armed forces, the Pentagon will be quick to advance military solutions while ignoring the most predictable fact of war—i.e., the inevitable, unintended consequences once bullets and bombs are given the green light. Arguably, that assumption is now more myth, as presidents on both sides of the aisle have often been the more aggressive advocates for a military response over the last seven decades.

The seven-decade, post–World War II period parallels the power of TV as the most effective microphone and real-time visual enjoyed by American presidents. Control of the powerful presidential *bully pulpit* is a very big deal. On a moment's notice, the president of the United States of America can be speaking to the world. Pause and reflect on that. Imagine yourself with that kind of power and the enormous responsibility to use it thoughtfully.

While the *Constitution* empowers the House of Representatives with the solemn authority to *declare* war, in 1973, Congress passed (over the veto of President Nixon) the *War Powers Act* that requires the president to *consult* with Congress before deploying the U.S. military in "hostilities" overseas.

This statutory mechanism provides a process for both the House *and* the Senate to debate and vote on the issue of deploying America's military to war-zone situations. As imperfect as the *War Powers Act* may be, it stands in stark contrast to the absolute power of dictators and autocrats, past and present.

Unlike the rapid response of *Operation Enduring Freedom* to the 9/11 attacks, the buildup to a war in Iraq, *Operation Iraqi Freedom*, was polarizing America with a tone and emotion reminiscent of Vietnam. While there was no military draft as had been the case during the Vietnam War, a proposed joint resolution (both the House and Senate), *Authorization for Use of Military Force Against Iraq Resolution of 2002*, became the focus of intense debate.

Against that backdrop, Maine's second district congressman, John Baldacci, was running for governor. And in an interview with me, he recalled how "politically difficult the *Resolution* was given the pro Iraq support of veterans groups and others."[9]

Together with Maine's first district congressman, Tom Allen, a meeting was arranged with Condoleezza Rice in an effort to be convinced of the presence of WMD. Baldacci remembers how "evasive" Rice was with no clear evidence to support the contention of WMD.

The meeting concluded with Baldacci and Allen emphasizing the need for "more proof." Lacking clear evidence of WMD, they both announced their opposition to the Resolution. Subsequently, back home in Maine, meetings and conference calls with veterans' groups and others were held to explain and defend their position. Their proactive response proved effective, as Baldacci was elected governor and Allen was reelected to Congress.

Reflecting on that period, Baldacci praised Bush "up to the time of Iraq," citing his presidential leadership on 9/11 and in the immediate days that followed "how he helped all of us, and how he handled the Taliban and al-Qaeda in Afghanistan."

Faced with the uncertainty of the looming midterm election in November and the possibility that the congressional balance of power in one or both houses could swing from Republican to Democratic control, the *Iraq Resolution* was approved, 373 to 156, on October 11, 2002. Maine's two senators, Olympia Snowe and Susan Collins, voted in support of the bipartisan resolution.

One month earlier, September 12, 2002, President Bush had addressed the United Nations General Assembly. The thrust of his speech was to call out the numerous times Saddam Hussein had defied United Nations resolutions, including those related to weapons systems and WMD. In his speech, Bush "urged the UN Security Council to act in the face of such repeated violations."[10]

On November 8, a few days after the U.S. midterm election, the UN Security Council, on a unanimous vote of 15–0, adopted Resolution 1441, giving Iraq "one final opportunity to comply with its disarmament obligations."[11]

There was little, if any doubt, that a phase-one military attack would not be successful. That confidence carried over as an assumption that the post-invasion capacity to manage the transition from the Hussein-led government to a provisional authority would be relatively smooth.

Among those who voiced such optimism on the outcome, one in particular stands out. Based on a meeting that Paul Wolfowitz had with Iraqi Americans in Detroit, Wolfowitz testified to the Senate Armed Services Committee, "I am reasonably certain that they will greet us as liberators and that will help us keep requirements down."[12] The prediction in itself served no useful purpose but to connect it to a conversation with Iraqi Americans in Detroit, Michigan, is astonishing.

In discussions leading up to war, the estimated post-invasion troop strength ranged from a Wolfowitz estimate of thirty-four thousand to General Shinseki estimating "several hundred thousand soldiers." In explaining his estimate to the Senate Armed Services Committee, Shinseki said "that Iraq was a large country with multiple ethnic tensions…so it takes significant ground force presence to ensure that people are fed, that water is distributed, all the normal responsibilities that go along with administering a situation like this."[13]

Missing from feel-good assumptions was an honest and candid acknowledgment of the unintended consequences that invariably surface in war. To that point, because Saddam Hussein was not quickly captured or killed in the invasion and the search for WMD continued without a finding, the rosy predictions of reduced troop strength proved to be a serious miscalculation.

Important in shaping a post-battlefield strategy would have been a candid acknowledgment that while some would see the United States as liberators, millions would also see us as invaders and occupiers. Is it not better to plan for both scenarios rather than assume the one that feels best?

During the period just before the March 2003 invasion, the former chief of the U.S. Central Command, Marine General Anthony Zinni, "became ever more convinced that interventionist neoconservative ideologues were plunging the nation into a war in a part of a world they didn't understand."[14] In that context, were we prepared for an undefined period to maintain the level of security needed for Iraq to evolve peacefully and miraculously embrace Western-style democracy?

In the eighteen months separating the October 2001 campaign in Afghanistan from the March 2003 invasion of Iraq, much attention was centered on the question of whether Iraq President Saddam Hussein was harboring weapons of mass destruction (WMD).

The dominance of the issue resulted in a false belief by many that Hussein was a coconspirator of the 9/11 attacks. Indeed, a *Guardian* poll in September 2003 found that close to 70 percent of Americans believed that Hussein was involved, thereby lending public support and legitimacy to the argument that military action in Iraq could wait no longer. Those in a position to clarify this misunderstanding evidently found it convenient to ignore the facts. In its July 22, 2004, report, *The 9/11 Commission* found no evidence that Saddam Hussein and al-Qaeda had an operational relationship.[15]

On February 5, 2003, shortly after the new Congress was sworn in, the administration called upon its most respected member, Secretary of State Colin Powell, to end the debate with a fact-filled speech to the United Nations attesting to the irrefutable fact of WMD in Iraq. Unlike those who were advocating for a military strike, Powell, a former four-star general, understood firsthand the law of unintended consequences that haunts every war.

Because of Powell's earlier misgivings about initiating a war in Iraq and the strong credibility he enjoyed with the media and the general public, he said to the world at the United Nations, "My colleagues, every statement I make today is backed up by sources, solid sources, adding, these are not assertions. What we are giving you are facts and conclusions based on solid intelligence."[16] Powell went on to describe in detail the intelligence that had been gathered in support of that conclusion. His presentation essentially sealed the deal.

As secretary of state, it was appropriate for Powell to make the case to the United Nations, but he would later say in an interview with Barbara Walters on *ABC News* that "the speech was a lasting blot on his record." Concluding that he was deliberately "misled" by the intelligence community, Powell openly said, "I am the one who presented it on behalf of the United States to the world."[17]

During the immediate weeks following the Powell UN speech, debate within the United Nations Security Council continued on a proposed new Resolution favored by the United States and Britain, two of the council's five permanent members. The other three permanent members (China, France, and Russia) together with the five nonpermanent members at that time (Angola, Chile, Germany, Pakistan, and Spain) opposed any language that could be used as an excuse for going to war. Thus, a majority of the Security Council opposed military action, believing that the United Nations–led inspection effort was comprehensive, well managed, and should be allowed to continue. Hussein, they argued, was being contained, so why rush into war?[18]

The debate was not confined to the United Nations or the halls of Congress. It spilled out across the world with hundreds of demonstrations against launching a war in Iraq. February 15, 2003, marked the peak of the protest with estimates of six to eleven million people gathered in 650 cities, thereby representing the largest international protest ever.[19]

For many in America, the war with Iraq was held up as a litmus test of patriotism, driving the emotions and passions that define differences of opinion in the public square. Fair enough, but democracy functions best when policy differences are debated respectfully and hopefully based more on fact than a feel-good, hoped-for outcome.

While that may be more aspirational than reality based, the growing prospect of war against Iraq added to the deepening polarization that had surfaced in the 2000 presidential election between George Bush and Al Gore. The fact that the outcome of that election was determined by one vote of the United States Supreme Court, stopping a recount of votes in Florida, served as an accurate barometer of the political divide. But to his credit, Gore immediately accepted the decision of the nation's highest court, thereby ensuring a peaceful transfer of power. While 9/11 had helped to reunite, the choice of war in Iraq reopened the breach.

Shock and awe

With the realization that a majority of the United Nations Security Council was at odds with the U.S. and British position, President Bush, Prime Minister Tony Blair, and Spain's prime minister, Jose Maria Aznar met in the Azores on March 16, 2003, to determine the next steps in the confrontation with Iraq. They were hosted by the Portuguese president, Jorge Sampaio. Britain and the United States were two of the five permanent members of the United Nations Security Council, and Spain was one of the nonpermanent members during that year.

At the close of their first meeting on March 16, Bush said they were "working toward the great cause of peace and security." Following their final meeting on March 17, Bush challenged Iraq's president, Saddam Hussein, to leave Iraq within forty-eight hours or face serious consequences.[20] In effect, he was drawing on United Nations Resolution 1441 and extending one last opportunity to Hussein to surrender.

As the hours ticked away, Hussein, dangling on a self-imposed death row, remained in defiance of the order. Bush would later write in his book, *Decision Points*, "On Wednesday, March 19, 2003, I walked in to a meeting I had hoped would not be necessary of the NSC [National Security Council] and gave the order to General Tommy Franks who was standing by at the Prince Sultan Air Base in Saudi Arabia along with the British and Australian defense teams."[21] Thus, on March 20, 2003 (March 21 in Iraq), the United States, together with Great Britain and its allied coalition, began the war in

Iraq with a massive "shock and awe" aerial attack directed at the Iraqi capital, Baghdad, and Mosul, the second-largest Iraqi city.[22]

In the context of the story of Chris and Lavi and the many others who were directly impacted by the impatience of a few to get on with a war whose outcome was assumed, is it not fair to ask what number of deaths, military and civilian, are "acceptable" to justify going to war? Was the decision to go to war reached through the filter of best case versus worst case, light casualties versus heavy casualties? How are those numbers calculated and measured in the justification for war? The final filter is the Achilles' heel, the inevitable lesson of war: its unintended consequences.

There is always a first and last to die in a war. And the pain of one death is felt as deeply by the affected family regardless of how many others are killed. Moreover, how are the hearts and minds of millions who live in a country under attack won over when the prospect of losing family along with the destruction of homes, buildings, and bridges becomes an everyday reality? Reasonable to ask, what is the calculus that supports such decisions?

One can imagine Chris and Lavi, newlyweds of less than a year, watching the skies as they lit up in the evening darkness of Iraq. From afar and in the comfort of our homes, death and destruction was disguised by the made-for-media, spectacular show of modern, advanced airpower, almost like watching an electronic game. Except it wasn't a game. The explosions we saw were the real thing. One moment, the screen shows a warehouse, for example. The next moment, it's gone—vaporized if you will—along with everything and anyone who may have been inside.

While they had no way of knowing that in less than a year, Chris would be in Mosul, along with the others of Maine's 133rd Engineering Battalion, it seems quite likely that they sat cuddled together, wondering what it might mean for them and others who were in the same situation. At that moment, Lavi would already be carrying the brunt of the emotional anxiety, while Chris, always the optimist, would be reassuring that everything would be okay.

Over the ensuing two weeks of OIF, some 1,700 sorties hit a multitude of targets in Iraq along with over five hundred Tomahawk cruise missiles launched from ships in the Persian Gulf and Red Sea. The air attacks in combination with a U.S.-led coalition of 177,000 troops took control of Baghdad, the Iraqi capital city, on April 9.[23]

But as relatively brief as the battle was, casualties are a fact of war, and in the three weeks of fighting, 172 coalition troops died, with 7,434 confirmed civilian deaths. While civilian populations may not be deliberately targeted, the fog of war inevitably results in the loss of innocent lives. Deaths by "direct violence," a term used to account for war-related violence by all parties, increased dramatically over the duration of the war.[24]

In the flush of a quick and decisive military victory as had been predicted, Bush copiloted a Navy fighter jet to the *USS Abraham Lincoln* just off the Southern California coast. With an enormous "*mission accomplished*" banner behind him, Bush declared, "Major combat operations in Iraq have ended." In recognizing the military accomplishment, he went on to say that "the tyrant has fallen, and Iraq is free."[25]

One can reasonably assume that the quick military success offered Chris and Lavinia and others in the same situation, reason to feel more confident of their future. Unfortunately, the hard, cold reality was that the search for Saddam Hussein's whereabouts would not be completed for another eight months. Each day that went by in the search for Hussein and parallel search for WMD stretched the capacity of the U.S. and coalition troops, thereby strengthening the insurgency. Declaring Iraq free was, at best, premature.

It soon became apparent that the scenario of insurgent forces as predicted earlier by Powell and other military and policy leaders had the look and feel of a long-term campaign, a campaign that conceivably might be measured in years if not decades. To that point, Chris's father, John Gelineau, wrote that when the Iraq War started, "all of us prayed for a swift end, so that Chris would not be deployed…but because the occupation did not end with Bush's announcement that the war had ended, it became apparent that more troops would be deployed."

If seasoned, experienced, career military leaders of the likes of Powell and General Shinsecki were trying to slow down a fast-moving train with patience, restraint, and contingency planning, would that not have been a more effective formula for achieving the larger goal?

And to be clear, when joining any branch of the military, including the National Guard, it is understood that you may be called to serve in a war zone or directed to respond to some other circumstance that puts you in harm's way. That's the deal. But the other part of the deal is to trust that your leaders will have exhausted all options in making the momentous decision that requires direct involvement, including the added filter required when activating National Guard units.

One does not need to be a pacifist or conscientious objector to raise these issues—I am neither—but going to war or authorizing military action should be the most sober, thoughtful decision for a government and its leaders to make. The commander in chief and his inner circle of advisers owe it to the troops in the field and their families that in reaching a decision to fight, all options have been fully and painstakingly vetted, including a realistic assessment of the post-battlefield mission to secure the peace. Conceding that my view may not reflect the process that was followed, there is little in the record to suggest otherwise.

The rush to judgment, the false narrative of urgency is difficult to understand in the context of American military power always available to call on in response to a clear and compelling situation. Combine that military strength with the acknowledgment that all leaders of nations enjoy their position of power and prestige more than anything else.

Ego rules, and it strains credulity that in the final analysis, Saddam Hussein would give up his power by initiating another unprovoked attack, especially with American military hovering over his shoulder, prepared to pounce like a tiger on a weak and dying dog. And he most certainly had not forgotten how quickly his forces were overtaken in 1991 by the United States and its multination coalition in the Gulf War.

IF YOU LOVE SOMEONE, YOU MUST TELL THEM

Historical perspective

The lens of history is a reflection of deliberate and naturally occurring events and consequences over time. Thus, fifteen years after the Gulf War, five years after 9/11, and three years after the 2003 invasion of Iraq, Pulitzer Prize–winning author, Thomas E. Ricks, provided an updated perspective on the war in Iraq.

In *Fiasco: The American Military Adventure in Iraq*, 2003 to 2005, Ricks maintained that, "The seeds to the second President Bush's decision to invade were planted by the unfinished nature of the 1991 war, in which the U.S. military expelled Iraq from Kuwait but ended the fighting prematurely and sloppily, without due consideration by the first President Bush and his advisers of what end state they wished to achieve."[26]

While acknowledging that the abrupt end of the 1991 Gulf War was seen by many as a prudent decision, that would keep America and its allied friends from being drawn into a long and costly war, Ricks posits that the rush to quickly end the Gulf War resulted in "three key mistakes," as summarized below in *Fiasco*.[27]

Mistake number 1. Shiites and Kurds were encouraged to rebel against Saddam Hussein but without U.S. support. Lacking that support was highlighted by General H. Norman Schwarzkopf's decision "in the euphoria of wars end, to approve an exception to the no-fly rule, to permit Iraqi helicopter flights—and Iraqi military helicopters were promptly used to shoot up the streets of the southern cities."

Mistake number 2. Because of the damage done to Saddam Hussein's regime, it was assumed that he would not survive as its leader.

Mistake number 3. Failure to "undercut" Hussein's military power, including the "elite Republican Guard units" who were allowed to leave Kuwait.

Hindsight is a beautiful thing, gifting rich material to historians, journalists, politicians, and regular people like me. Fair to speculate, if President George H. W. Bush had made sure that Hussein's regime was over at the end of the Gulf War, would Iraq with all its historic factions transition to a more open and stable society?

In such a scenario, it's possible that Iraq may have been spared the crippling economic sanctions that plagued the country during Hussein's final decade in power. But given the dynamic of a power vacuum in the office of president, how would a consensus candidate be chosen? Because it's impossible to know what unintended consequences would have resulted from such a hypothetical scenario, a peaceful transfer of power should not be assumed.

The "key mistakes" cited by Ricks are factually based and provide relevant context to the events that would follow a decade later.

Because Iraq remained unfinished business, U.S. policy leaders essentially fell into two camps: a policy of continued containment or a policy of proactive regime change.

With the conclusion of the 1991 Gulf War, a process to monitor Hussein's regime coupled with continued economic sanctions was adopted by the United Nations Security Council. *Resolution 687* also defined the terms of the cease-fire and established a United Nations Special Commission (UNSCOM) to establish a process for determining whether Iraq had WMD and if so, to ensure that those weapons would be destroyed along with the capacity to continue such programs.

During the eight-year period of UNSCOM, Saddam Hussein was less than fully cooperative. While his obstinance was predictable, it was reported in the September 2004 *Duelfer Report* that "he did not want to leave the impression with Iran's Shiite rulers that his regime was weak militarily and [for them] to see opportunity for revenge."[28]

Consequently, the *Duelfer Report* suggested that rather than comply with the United Nations resolution, Hussein had quietly destroyed his biological and chemical weapons. According to David Kay, who led the Iraq Survey Group effort to find WMD, if the *Duelfer* report was accurate, Hussein presumably concluded that maintaining the image of strength within the region was of higher priority than risking the loss of his presidency, which would certainly result if WMD were found.

Perhaps Hussein also reasoned that if it was proved that he did not have WMD, it would be all the easier for a U.S.-led coalition to bring him down. The mere threat that he had stockpiles of WMD gave him leverage both regionally and globally. This is not to defend Hussein, but it does offer one possible explanation of the calculus behind his decision to engage in a high-risk game of roulette.

With the closure of UNSCOM in 1998, President Clinton ordered a four-day bombing of Iraq beginning on December 16 of that year. Under the code name *Desert Fox*, the brief campaign was viewed by some as more PR than substance. And yet as described by Thomas Ricks in *Fiasco*, "a total of 415 cruise missiles…and 600 bombs had hit 97 sites, the major ones being facilities for the production and storage of chemical weapons and those associated with missiles that could deliver such munitions…the strikes also hit government command and control facilities, such as intelligence and secret police headquarters."

At the time of the Desert Fox strikes, Marine General Anthony Zinni was serving as the chief U.S. Central Command. Ricks reports in *Fiasco* how "Zinni was amazed when Western intelligence assets in Baghdad reported that Desert Fox nearly knocked off Saddam Hussein's regime" and how Zinni concluded that "Containment is clearly working, and Saddam Hussein was on the ropes."[29]

In a February 11, 2004, updated article in *The National Security Archive* of December 1998, it was reported that "UNSCOM withdrew from Iraq in the face of Iraqi refusal to cooperate, and harassment." With a new president in 2001, George W. Bush said in the same article that "the U.S. made it clear that it would not accept what had become the status quo with respect to Iraq." Accordingly, and after considerable negotiations within the United Nations Security Council, "the United Nations declared that Iraq would have to accept even more intrusive inspections than under the previous regime." Faced with the reality of no advantageous option, Saddam Hussein agreed to the new process.[30]

With Vice President Cheney and the civilian political appointee leaders of the Bush administration beating the drums for war, Ricks writes in *Fiasco* of the "Persistent doubts at the Pentagon…of the wisdom of invading Iraq and about adopting a policy of preemption." The Pentagon doubters sided with General Zinni's assessment of a few years earlier that the results of Operation Desert Fox suggested that containment was working. In advocating for continued containment, Zinni added that "it wasn't a particularly costly effort…we contained day-to-day, with fewer troops than go to work every day at the Pentagon."[31]

The Coalition Provisional Authority

The flames of the insurgency were fanned by a number of decisions and miscalculations that were largely rooted in the office of the secretary of defense, Donald Rumsfeld, in close coordination with Vice President Cheney and his top staff. Of significance was the appointment of former Ambassador L. Paul "Jerry" Bremer replacing Retired Army Lieutenant General Jay Garner as chief of the *Coalition Provisional Authority* (CPA).[32]

With the government of Iraq sidelined and President Saddam Hussein on the lamb, the CPA essentially became the government of Iraq. As Ricks writes in *Fiasco*, shortly after arriving in Baghdad on May 13, 2003 (seven months before the 133rd would deploy), "Bremer quickly made three moves that radically altered the American approach to Iraq and went a long way toward creating support for anti-American insurgency."[33]

Garner, who would leave Iraq within three days of Bremer arriving, was "appalled" with Bremer's *de-Ba'athification order. Coalition Provisional Authority Order Number 1* purged "tens of thousands of Baath Party members, perhaps as many as eighty-five thousand," many of whom were holding important positions in education, medicine, and the critical infrastructure of power plants, roads, and bridges.[34]

A week later, Bremer issued *CPA Order Number 2: Dissolution of Iraqi Entities*, which included armed forces, police and domestic security forces, and presidential security units. All told, Ricks found that the two CPA orders "threw out of work more than half a million people and alienated many more dependent on those lost incomes." Bremer's military liaison, Army Colonel John Agoglia of Central Command, told Bremer, "You guys just blindsided CENTCOM," and he would later characterize the action as the day "that we snatched defeat from the jaws of victory and created an insurgency."[35]

CPA Order Number 3 by Bremer was an announcement that despite Garner's plan, there would not be an Iraqi government for some time. At about the same time, Bremer added more woes to middle-class workers by shutting down unprofitable government run industries.[36] Arguably, from a financial perspective, closure may have been a defensible decision, but the timing could not have been worse, as it amplified the shrinking job opportunities for Iraqi citizens. One of the lessons of history is that punishing a defeated population with large-scale unemployment is a cruel and counterproductive policy.

While it is fair to ask what the process was in developing the CPA orders and the role Bremer played in shaping those policies, Ricks writes in *Fiasco* that the three CPA orders "contradicted the decisions made by President Bush on March 10 and 12 at briefings on postwar Iraq, according to an administration official who participated in both."[37] Regardless of Bremer's role in crafting the CPA orders, the focus that General Zinni and Lieutenant General Jay Garner had initiated that the United States would facilitate and support the involvement of Iraqis in rebuilding their communities was reversed by the administration.

The CPA orders represented significant policy decisions that presumably would have involved Cheney and Rumsfeld and their top staff with the back of the president. To that point, in his book, *Decision Points*, George W. Bush wrote, "In retrospect, I should have insisted on more debate on Jerry's orders, especially on what message disbanding the army would send and how many Sunnis the de-Baathification would affect."[38]

In addition to the CPA orders, each of which resulted in enormous negative impacts on the daily lives of the Iraqi population, the obsession to find WMD inadvertently provided huge caches of armaments to the insurgent effort.

To draw again on the exhaustive research of Ricks, he writes in *Fiasco*, "In bunkers across Iraq there were tens of thousands of tons of conventional weaponry—mortar shells, RPG's, rifle ammunition, explosives, and so on… Yet U.S. commanders rolling into

Iraq refrained from detonating those bunkers for fear that they also contained stockpiles of poison gas or other weaponry that might be blown into the air and kill U.S. soldiers or Iraqi civilians...so the bunkers often were bypassed and left undisturbed by an invasion force that already was stretched thin—and the insurgents were able to arm themselves at leisure... The US focus on WMD also provided a smokescreen of sorts, that unintentionally protected the insurgents during the spring of 2004."[39]

The relative ease by insurgent forces to gain access to conventional weapons bolstered the credibility of military leaders like Major General James Mattis, who at the onset advocated the need for additional troops in a post-invasion Iraq.

It also begs the question of planning and how a significant inventory of weaponry was allowed to exist in numerous locations throughout Iraq without a comprehensive management, security, and containment plan. Arguably, too, it stretches the logic of having inspected numerous bunkers, only to conclude that there "might be" stockpiles of poison gas, and therefore, we will simply leave the site. If that's what happened, where was the common sense filter in that decision?

The example of the accessible weapons bunkers is difficult to understand given the priority to confirm WMD while also being prepared and ready to confront the insurgency. It seems emblematic of so many other issues of preparedness during this period. Recognizing that these findings are specific to the first two years of Operation Iraqi Freedom further serves to question whether the United States and its Coalition partners were fully prepared to deal with the unintended consequences of the decision to invade Iraq when they did.

Writing of the war, Ricks summarized it succinctly:

> It is a tragedy in which every major player contributed to the errors, but in which the heroes tend to be anonymous and relatively powerless—the frontline American soldier doing his best in a difficult situation, the Iraqi civilian, trying to care for a family amid chaos and violence. They are the people who pay every day with blood and tears for the failures of high officials and powerful institutions.[40]

IF YOU LOVE SOMEONE, YOU MUST TELL THEM

---

1. The Baltimore Sun (by *New York Times* news service), *Bush Envisions a Marshall Plan for Afghanistan* (April 18, 2022).
2. Frederick Barton, *Peace Works: America's Unifying Role in a Turbulent World*, 10–11.
3. Clarke, *Against All Enemies*, 30.
4. *The President's News Conference* (www.govinfo.gov, July 8, 2002, 1190).
5. Ricks, *Fiasco*, 48.
6. Ibid. 49.
7. Ibid. 50–51.
8. Ibid. 82–83.
9. John E. Baldacci, *telephone interview with author* (August 30, 2019).
10. George W. Bush, *Speech to the United Nations General Assembly* (September 12, 2002).
11. *United Nations Security Council Resolution* 1441.
12. Ricks, *Fiasco*, 98.
13. Ibid. 97, 98.
14. Ibid. 87.
15. *The 9/11 Commission Report* (July 22, 2004).
16. Ricks, *Fiasco*, 90, 91.
17. Steven R. Weisman, "Powell Calls His UN Speech A Lasting Blot on His Record," *New York Times* (September 9, 2005).
18. United Nations Security Council and the Iraq War.
19. *The Largest Protest Ever Was 15 Years Ago* (www.huffpost.com, February 15, 2018).
20. George W. Bush, *Address to the Nation on Iraq* (March 17, 2003).
21. George W. Bush, *Decision Points*, 223.
22. Ricks, *Fiasco*, 117.
23. Wikipedia, *Invasion of Iraq*.

24. *Iraq Body Count Project* (up to April 30, 2003. Also, Watson Institute of International and Public Affairs, Brown University, *Costs of War*).
25. Wikipedia, *Casualties of the Iraq War* (by month).
26. George W. Bush, *Announces End of Major Combat Operations in Iraq* (AmericanRhetoric.com, delivered on May 1, 2003, from the *USS Abraham Lincoln* off the coast of San Diego, California).
27. Ricks, *Fiasco*, 5.
28. Ibid. 5.
29. Ibid. 375–377.
30. Ibid. 18–22.
31. The National Security Archive, *Iraq and Weapons of Mass Destruction* (edited by Jeffrey Michelson, updated on February 11, 2004).
32. Ricks, *Fiasco*, 20–22.
33. Ibid. 155.
34. Ibid. 160.
35. Ibid. 163.
36. Ibid. 165.
37. Ricks, *Fiasco*, 155.
38. George W. Bush, *Decision Points*.
39. Ricks, *Fiasco*, 145.
40. Ibid. 4.

Off to Iraq

A special good bye gift from Chris

CHAPTER 7

The 133rd Deployed to Iraq

IN A NOVEMBER 16, 2003, EMAIL TO family and friends, Lavinia wrote that Chris "had received a deployment order." Soon thereafter, he began to train full time with the Maine Army Reserve National Guard (MEARNG) 133rd Engineering Battalion. On December 7, 2003, the date of the 1941 Pearl Harbor attacks, the 133rd was formally activated for *Operation Iraqi Freedom II*.

With deployment orders in hand, Chris and his fellow soldiers likely reflected on how it came to be that their decision to join the National Guard was now leading them to a war in Iraq. Ever since they signed up, they knew the consequence of that decision could lead to a war zone. However, some like Specialist Chris Gelineau, who signed up while still in high school and prior to 9/11, believed it was unlikely that they would be deployed to a war. Regardless, the speculation that started on 9/11 was now a confirmed reality that carried with it personal impacts on family and careers.

Although money, educational support, and other benefits were significant reasons to join the Guard, some whom I interviewed also cited 9/11 as a motivating event behind their decision. According to former Maine National Guard, Brigadier General Libby, most of those who joined after 9/11 did so with the expectation of deployment to the Middle East. Others who joined, Libby being a prime example, had previously served in a branch of the military full time.[1]

According to the 133rd Battalion commander, John Jansen, there are "federal budgetary and operational benefits" realized by using National Guard and Reserve personnel in combination with regular military. In addition to the operational assets, the economic benefits to the region and state are significant through payroll, education support, and local vendor services.

Among the lessons learned from Vietnam, Jansen contends that it was a "mistake" to not activate Guard and Reserve units during that period. The heavy reliance on the military draft to meet the battlefield needs in Vietnam proved to be a policy with lasting negative consequences. And it certainly added to the controversy of the war and the unwelcome return many soldiers faced back in the states. Jansen points out that the "doctrine" defining the military approach to Vietnam changed in the 1980s and was implemented in the relatively brief 1990 through 1991 Gulf War. He maintains that "integrating guard and reserve components with regular military builds greater state-wide and community awareness and support to all service members."

I would agree that from an operational perspective, the age differentials, experience, and career backgrounds of Guard and Reserve soldiers adds important diversity, expertise, and camaraderie to each unit. The structure builds on the common bond of living and working in the same region and can add an intangible ingredient to the level of a unit's teamwork and competence. In contrast, the Army fighting in Vietnam was a combination of volunteer enlistees, commissioned officers, and significant numbers of drafted soldiers. Very few National Guard or Reservists were deployed to Vietnam. And because of that policy, openings in either option were scarce.

I can relate to the Vietnam era draft but make no claim of serving there. Suddenly faced with the likelihood of being drafted, I fulfilled my obligation by enlisting in the Coast Guard. I was training as a helicopter crewman when a medical condition sidelined me to radio communications. While being hospitalized at Saint Albans Naval Hospital in Queens, New York, patients included returning soldiers from Vietnam, and for reasons that were sometimes obvious, their conditions were far more extreme than mine. I often wonder how many of those guys were able to transition back to a healthy and forward-thinking life.

Tragically, over the years, we have witnessed and often without realizing, Vietnam vets among the homeless. Many have passed away by now, but some still stand or sit at street corners, disheveled and lost, quietly asking for help. Their numbers now include veterans from our decades-long Middle East wars. "Home" is a tarp tucked under a bridge or strung around some bushes in a wooded or abandoned area of town. Being killed on the battlefield is just one metric of war.

Iraqi freedom II

In the Bush administration war planning, a second phase, *Iraqi Freedom II,* had been integrated with the overall plan. The second phase would follow the military invasion and hoped for swift capture of Saddam Hussein. Achieving the latter was critical to the objective of transitioning from a brutal dictatorship to an open and citizen-based government. To the extent possible, the humanitarian mission of community support was carried out as time and resources allowed. But supporting the military effort—securing peace—continued to be the highest priority of the 133rd and all other military units in Iraq.

While the attack on Iraq in March of 2003 had achieved its initial objective, the resultant insurgency, intensified by Bremer's CPA orders, was more effective and widespread than anticipated by President Bush and his team. Consequently, the declaration, "Mission accomplished," telegraphed a false and premature conclusion, thereby making it all the more necessary for continued aggressive military operations.

Jansen put it succinctly, "Things were progressing nicely after the initial conflict, but when he [Bremer] gave no hope for a prosperous future for the people who had a lot to lose [Ba'th party folks], and by dismantling the Iraq army and other security entities to include the police, he allowed a huge security vacuum, thus creating a wild-west like atmosphere that allowed for insurgent and other nefarious groups to settle in."

IF YOU LOVE SOMEONE, YOU MUST TELL THEM

The capture of Saddam Hussein

On December 13, 2003, six days after the formal activation of the 133rd and eight months since the start of the invasion, Saddam Hussein was captured by U.S. troops. After twenty-four years of living in the regal splendor of numerous palaces, Hussein was found dirty and disheveled, hiding in an eight-foot-deep hole in the town of ad-Dawr, nine miles from his hometown of Tikrit.

Under the code name *Red Dawn*, a force of six hundred troops had been searching relentlessly with a determination akin to the search for WMD. In the end, the capture was the work of many. In particular, though, Army Staff Sergeant Eric Maddox proved to be the driving force in learning of Hussein's whereabouts.[2] He was meticulous and comprehensive in staying with a nonviolent process that required extraordinary persistence in the interrogation of hundreds of detainees.

Of relevance to the insurgency and the events that swept the 133rd and thousands of others into war, if Hussein had been captured early in the invasion, as the plan called for, that would have altered the dynamic of events in Iraq. In addition to the hope of finding WMD, removal of Hussein from office was the other major reason for invading the country. The intense high-priority search for Hussein and the equally intense parallel search for WMD undoubtedly diverted resources and strategic focus from the post-invasion priority to first secure the peace. Instead, the fog of war fueled the energy of the insurgency as many military leaders had predicted. Whether he realized it or not, Hussein's ability to avoid capture for eight months was a significant source of that fuel.

Preparing for Iraq

On January 6, 2004, the 133rd was transferred from Maine to Fort Drum in Upstate New York for more intensive training prior to being sent directly to Iraq. And at about the same time, Maine's 152nd Field Artillery unit mobilized to Iraq. Consisting of 124 soldiers, the 152nd was assigned to guard the infamous Abu Ghraib prison on the outer edge of Iraq's capital city, Baghdad. The story of the 152nd is graphically told by Portland, Maine, author W. Zach Griffith in his book, *Packed for the Wrong Trip*.[3]

The 152nd was assigned to the prison after horrendous media reports of torture and human rights violations on Iraqi detainees by U.S. Army soldiers and the CIA. The violations had far-reaching consequences and added emotional fuel to the intense insurgency. Maine's 152nd performed with compassion and competence in restoring a sense of decency and order to the prison.

The January 6 departure of the 133rd to Fort Drum was its formal send-off from Maine. As described by Justin Ellis of the *Portland Press Herald*, the send-off was "the largest deployment of National Guard Troops from Maine since World War II."[4] As the battalion bordered buses for Fort Drum, a photographer captured the moment with a picture of Lavinia and Chris as they embraced. They would see each other one more time before the 133rd went to Iraq, ironically on that most romantic of days, Valentine's Day.

That Lavinia and Chris would be featured in the send-off article of the 133rd reflects the energy of their love and how it radiated and drew others to their orbit. In its simplicity, the photograph captured the pain of deep love when it comes face to face with war, a theme that has played out for centuries and more. Lavinia's riveting dark eyes and Chris's youthful promise are the universal language that generations of all ages understand. Words just get in the way. The picture says it all.

The 133rd would spend the next six weeks in training at Fort Drum before heading to Iraq. During this period, on January 24, 2004, National Security Adviser Condoleezza Rice conceded that no WMD had been found. David Kay, the chief weapons inspector, resigned and testified the same message to Congress, saying, "We were almost all wrong."[5]

Reporting from Fort Drum on February 8, Bill Nemitz of the *Maine Sunday Telegram* wrote a lengthy piece, "Bracing for Iraq."[6] In describing the training that the troops from Maine had gone through, Battalion Commander Jansen said, "Everything we've asked these people to do, they've taken seriously. They want to do the right thing—and they want to learn."

In that same article, Jansen summarized that the community building piece will be either "horizontal" (rebuilding roads, bridges, and other parts of Iraq's battered infrastructure) or "vertical" (erecting schools, hospitals, and other much-needed buildings). While part of the mission as described by Jansen was inherently a peaceful and humanitarian initiative, it was also clearly understood that they would be in a war zone with all the potential for violence from insurgent forces who did not want a U.S. presence in their country. The prospect of being a "target" prompted Captain Michael Mitchell, commander of the 133rd's Charlie Company, to say that "it weighs on me a great deal… I want to bring everyone back alive."

Mosul, Iraq

As noted earlier, the geographic size of Iraq is roughly equivalent to that of California. According to Jansen, the area of operations for the 133rd centered in the northeast region of Iraq and included the Kurdistan regions of Irbil to the east, bordering Iran; Dohuk to the north, bordering Turkey; and Nineveh to the west, bordering Syria. For context, the 133rd's area of responsibility covered over fifty-eight thousand square miles, an area roughly equivalent to a region that would stretch from Philadelphia to Boston and with a population of 4.5 million.

Encircling the ancient city of Nineveh, the city of Mosul lies 250 miles north of Baghdad and serves as the capital of the Nineveh Province. Originally, Mosul occupied the west bank of the Tigris River, but as the city grew, it expanded to include Nineveh on the east bank. For centuries, Mosul has provided an important crossing point on the Tigris (1,300 miles long and twenty-seven feet deep) for commerce between the Mediterranean and Indian Oceans. To the west of the Tigris flows the Euphrates, the longest river in West Asia (1,740 miles and up to 750 feet deep). Both rivers weave a path through Iraq from the mountains of Turkey to the Persian Gulf and have played a vital role in the life and culture of the country over the centuries.[7]

Camp Marez

The 133rd was assigned to the First U.S. Corps Task Force Olympia (TFO) in the Multinational Brigade Northwest

(MNB-NW) area of operations (AO) under Commanding General Carter F. Ham, brigadier general of the United States Army.[8]

Camp Marez became the forward operating base (FOB) of the 133rd. Located on a large tract of land near the Mosul Airfield, FOB Marez had functioned under various names prior to the arrival of the 133rd and had also served as the home to some units of the 101st Airborne Division.

All but 22 of the 571 men and women of the 133rd were headquartered at FOB Marez and organized as the Headquarters Support Company (HSC). The HSC, commanded by Captain Michael Steinbuchel, was one of four companies reporting to Battalion Commander Jansen. The other three companies were Alpha, Bravo, and Charlie. Thus, FOB Marez served as a departure point for squads, platoons, and at times, entire companies as they executed missions across the area of operations for days, weeks, and months at a time.

The twenty-two soldiers not headquartered at FOB Marez, including Specialist Chris Gelineau and Battalion Commander Jansen, were assigned to the battalion command at *Camp Freedom*, often referred to as the "Palace." Located in the urban center of Mosul, five miles from FOB Marez, the Palace was one of numerous opulent personal residences used by Saddam Hussein in Iraq.

While the principal duties of the battalion command were administrative, all members of the battalion were soldiers first and required to participate in external operations in order to meet the needs of the overall mission.

Conditions on arrival

In an effort to better understand the conditions on the ground when the 133rd arrived in Iraq, below are questions that I asked of Battalion Commander Jansen:

> NA—Was the mission size that the 133rd covered, an area roughly comparable to New York City to Boson, realistic? Was Washington overconfident?

JJ—I would agree that Washington was overconfident of the results. The Army was not designed to take over and secure such a large area for a protracted amount of time. When we arrived we replaced the 101st Airborne Division which at that time, with attached units, had somewhere between 25,000 and 30,000 troops.

Task Force Olympia, the task force I was part of, was a brigade plus and had eight thousand troops that grew toward the end with the increased threat. The initial plan, based on expectations that things were going to go well, was to replace our task force with a battalion plus, maybe one thousand soldiers, and then quickly remove all troops and turn it over to the Iraqis. This seemed possible at the start. When we arrived, things were going pretty good and moving in a good direction. In my opinion, because of key mistakes at the highest level, things became worse, preventing the original plan from becoming reality.

NA—Describe the conditions in Mosul when the 133rd arrived.

JJ—Mosul and surrounding areas were mostly intact when we arrived. Overall though the infrastructure was in rough shape but not necessarily because of combat operations. The one thing I noticed was that the US is very good at targeting (not perfect) especially from the air. The heavy damage that I saw was to facilities connected with the Iraq military and Saddam's regime. Every Iraqi military base had extensive damage as well as a number of buildings in the Palace complex and other government buildings. There were also several residential neighborhoods in Mosul that I noticed had extensive damage. One of these was Giziani Village next to FOB Marez.

NA—What were some of the big issues you had to deal with?

JJ—One of the biggest issues was looting. When the regime fell and the Iraqi army and security forces left their posts looting became rampant. I remember talking to the Commander I replaced and he was telling me how there was a race to get to Mosul to protect infrastructure. It took only a few days to get there but by the time the US and Coalition forces arrived most of the government buildings had been looted. The looters stripped just about anything they thought had value or could be used to include, windows, doors, fixtures, furniture, electrical wires in the walls, plumbing. Even when we were there if a building was vacant it would be immediately stripped.

NA—How about critical infrastructure?

JJ—It was the goal, prior to and after initial combat operations, not to destroy critical infrastructure that was needed post combat operations. I think overall the damage to critical infrastructure was minimized and there was significant effort to improve what was there following initial combat operations. Unfortunately what was needed to be done because of neglect and lack of investment over a long period was overwhelming. The Iraqi's at first seemed excited we were there and expected that we could fix everything in their country overnight but that was just not possible.

NA—What were the systemic infrastructure issues in Mosul?

JJ—The electrical grid was terrible and there were rolling blackouts. I think the people may have averaged about 4 hours of power per day. Water and sewerage was also a problem, but it looked like it had been a problem for a long time. Construction was pretty shoddy and we often said we're in the land of "not quite right." Structures would look ok on the surface, but underneath the facades it was awful. For example, the palace had beautiful exotic stone mosaics on the outside and behind them, crumbling substandard concrete.

NA—Was there any evidence of damage to destruction of historic buildings and cultural sites?

JJ—It was a high priority to ensure that these special places were not disturbed or damaged. With one exception, I was not aware of any damage to historic and cultural sites. The one exception that I was aware of was someone from the 101st Airborne Division painted some Screaming Eagle logos on a historic site and the 133rd ended up removing them.

Tragically, after the 133rd left, ISIS destroyed most of the historic and cultural sites in the city. It is very unfortunate since the city has such an amazing history and had numerous significant historic sites. One of the sites, the Dar Mar Elia Monastery, was located on FOB Marez. It was constructed in the late sixth century by Assyrian Christian monks and for centuries, served as the a center for Christian life where pilgrims would come in November to celebrate the Feast of Saint Elijah. Another well-known site was the tomb and mosque of the prophet Jonah, which was destroyed by ISIS. Unfortunately, that is just the tip of the iceberg. Hundreds of historic sites have been destroyed since we pulled out.

IF YOU LOVE SOMEONE, YOU MUST TELL THEM

You fight with what you have

A major disappointment to Jansen and the troops of the 133rd was a directive from Washington that all the equipment of the 133rd was to remain in Maine, equipment that prompted Jansen to say, "We've taken a lot of pride over the years in picking up and maintaining the equipment that we have…but there's nothing we can do. It's not coming with us." According to Nemitz of the *Portland Press Herald*, this included all "state-of-the-art trucks, bull dozers and other heavy equipment, widely viewed as one of the country's newest and best maintained National Guard engineering fleets."

When I queried Maine National Guard Adjutant General Bill Libby regarding the equipment issue, he suggested a big factor may have been the logistics of transferring multiple numbers of vehicles and equipment from the Persian Gulf at Kuwait and moving it seven hundred miles to Mosul in northern Iraq.

As the 133rd soon discovered the equipment awaiting them in Iraq was inferior to what they had been ordered to leave behind. As described by Lieutenant Adam Cote, the Humvees that the battalion inherited lacked any reinforced steel and in the context of the battlefield, were so flimsy that the only option available, for a time, was to duct tape flak jackets to the doors and lay bags of sand on the vehicle floor to help cushion the impact of an improvised explosive device (IED).

My incredulous response to Cote was "Are you kidding me?" The strongest military machine in the world sends the nations men and women to fight a war in Iraq, and in order to improve the safety of their vehicles, the units in the field were on their own. The Band-Aids of choice included scrounging for scrap steel and duct taping flak jackets on thin-skinned vehicle doors. A negative to the sandbags was the added weight to the vehicle, thereby reducing its ability to move as fast as designed. Ultimately, the Army developed up-armor kits for the Humvees (High Mobility Multipurpose Wheeled Vehicles). While the kits helped to improve the safety of the Humvee, they were not a panacea.

According to Jansen, the added weight of the kits on first-generation Humvees required the replacement of all engines and suspension systems on the battalion's entire Humvee fleet, an effort that Jansen described as an "amazing feat." Jansen praised Sergeant Lynn Poulin, an experienced mechanic and shipbuilder at Bath Iron Works for the "instrumental role" he played in directing the modifications to the vehicles, adding, "I was truly blessed as a commander to have so many soldiers like Lynn who were determined to do anything they could to protect their fellow soldiers."

Inferior equipment was a widespread issue throughout Iraq and was a significant cause in many of the tragic and unnecessary deaths and injuries of soldiers. This was especially so during the early period of the war, before more battle designed vehicles were deployed. That strikes me as a consequence that should have been anticipated in the decision to go to war, given the Gulf War experience and the subsequent ongoing tensions leading up to 9/11.

To that point, how much time and consideration was given to worst-case scenarios that the soldiers in the field would be faced with? Or was the lack of preparation driven more from a belief that the outcome would be swift and successful? The assumptions of a swift conclusion reinforce my view that the cautionary voices of a possible insurgency were not taken as seriously as those in power should have.

The work of the 133rd

A compelling way to summarize the mission and work of the 133rd Maine Army Engineering Battalion is to draw from a lengthy *Recommendation for the Meritorious Unit Commendation 10* as submitted by Brigadier General Carter Ham to the commander of the Multi-National Forces in Iraq, who at that time was General John Abizaid. Below is a summary of commendation highlights.

> The 133rd Engineer Combat Battalion is recommended for the *Army Meritorious Unit Commendation* in recognition of its extraordinary performance during mobilization and

deployment to Iraq in support of Operation Iraqi Freedom II from March 04–27 to February 05. The 133rd displayed outstanding devotion and superior performance of exceptionally difficult and diverse tasks so as to set itself apart from all other combat heavy engineer units in theater.

Serving as both an engineer battalion supporting the Area of Operations (AO) and as the Task Force Engineer, the 133rd provided much-needed support to the Iraqi people, all branches of the Iraqi Security Force (ISF), and Multi-National Forces. As Task Force Engineer, the 133rd tracked all AO military and civilian engineer missions, ASP clearance operations, minefield database upkeep, and infrastructure improvement projects to host nation contractors in excess of $15 million.

In its role as a combat heavy engineering battalion, the 133rd completed over 730 troop missions on every Multinational Forward Operating Base and for every branch of the ISF. Their efforts included missions on the Syrian, Turkish, and Iranian borders, airfield maintenance, runway restoration, construction of forts, towers, berms and critical electrical assessments and repairs.

Humanitarian relief was also provided to Iraqi citizens in the form of computers, school supplies, generators, food and clothing. On their own initiative, the 133rd identified and completed 84 humanitarian assistance missions in the Irbil and Dahuk Provinces and working with California, Civil Affairs Battalions repaired or constructed schools, clinics, community centers, roads, and culverts.

IF YOU LOVE SOMEONE, YOU MUST TELL THEM

The battalion commander

It takes a team to be successful, and it takes a leader to build a team. In the spirit of the proud motto of the 133rd, *To the Last Man*, John Jansen exemplified the best qualities of leadership: disciplined, competent, and compassionate. Jansen is of the stripe of a ship captain who will be the last to leave a sinking ship.

In promoting Lieutenant Colonel John Jansen to serve as the battalion commander, the 133rd could not have been better served as evidenced through General Ham's ringing recommendation for the Meritorious Unit Commendation.

The general's merit-based recognition of the 133rd did not single out one individual but deliberately recognized the entirety of the 133rd, all 577 men and women who worked as a team to fulfill the mission they were assigned. When egos are parked at the door, it's amazing what a group can accomplish. That said, whether a group of five or five hundred, success in any organization starts at the top with a leader who understands the critical importance of building trust and confidence through clear and consistent communications, qualities that are amplified in their importance when leading a battalion in an always-dangerous and unpredictable theater of war environment.

Jansen brought these and other positive leadership qualities to his position as the battalion commander. His empathy and sensitivity to the women and men he led during their deployment to Iraq was quietly demonstrated in the immediate days following the horrific December 21, 2004, suicide terrorist attack at the Camp Marez mess tent. (see page 133) It was Christmastime, far from everyone's home in Maine. Jansen chose to spend the next few nights away from the Palace where he was headquartered and instead bunk with the soldiers at FOB Marez. Those soldiers knew their battalion commander had their back. That sense of duty and commitment would be tested to the very end of the battalion's deployment at Fort Drum.

My first meeting with John Jansen was on April 6, 2019. With his Lab, Buddy, curled up at his feet, we met in the 1904 summer cottage that Jansen and his wife, Rae-Lynn, purchased in 2015. Over that period, they have done a masterful job in restoring the classic

Maine lakeside cottage. With a tasteful blend of updates that retain the charm of the past with the efficiency and appeal of contemporary style and design, a warm and special home is the result.

Sitting comfortably in the winterized front porch and gazing out at the mushy ice on Lake Cobbosseecontee (Wabenaki for "plenty of sturgeon"), my mind quickly fixed on the stark contrast between the peaceful world in front and the chaotic world that Jansen left behind in Iraq, a world and a time he will never forget.

John Jansen's path of decades-long service in the National Guard followed the route many others have taken to blend service to one's country with support for higher education. Born in Boston, Jansen joined the Guard in March of 1980 under the Simultaneous Membership Program that he was accepted at the University of Maine in Orono (UMO). He earned a bachelor in arts degree in economics from UMO while receiving his commission in 1983 and would later go on to earn a master's of strategic studies from the United States Army War College.

Over the ensuing years, Jansen continued to seek advanced training and education opportunities to further his career. Those efforts and his commitment to excellence positioned him well for a number of high-level leadership assignments. The quality and dedication of his work is reflected in the numerous awards and recognitions that he received over the years. Following his service in Iraq and after thirty years of military service, Jansen retired from the National Guard in 2013 with the rank of colonel. Athletic and trim through regular rowing on the lake and biking on the backroads of Maine, Jansen serves as the superintendent of the Waterville, Maine, Sewerage District.

My conversation with Jansen stretched for over two hours and touched on a range of issues regarding his career in the military and the challenging year in which he served as the battalion commander of Maine's 133rd.

Always quick to praise, he attributed the success of the unit to the quality of the men and women whom he was privileged to lead, noting that the blend of young and old and the diversity of professional skills and life experiences provide the National Guard with a more balanced and grounded force than military units built from the all-volunteer Army or the selective service draft. Jansen added that financially, utilizing the National Guard is less expensive to the American taxpayer than the cost of maintaining only a full-time, regular military.

In real-time military operations, the chain of command structure that integrates National Guard units with the regular Army appears to work effectively when the respective leaders of each branch are of the quality and stature of Colonel John Jansen and Brigadier General Carter Ham, commander of operation of Iraqi Freedom's National Task Force Olympia–North. Jansen considers Ham the "smartest person I have ever known, an excellent listener with an exceptional ability to compartmentalize the enormous range of responsibilities and decisions that he had to deal with each day."

Jansen marveled at Ham's ability to cut right to a decision that was logical, fact based, and always consistent with the larger purpose of the mission. A clear example being how quickly Ham signaled his support for the humanitarian plan developed by the 133rd to build good will in the towns and villages of their area of operations. In doing so, he sent a strong signal that the larger objective of the mission is to not just win on the battlefield but to be a positive force in building community. Community building and relationships were not just window dressing but important strategic initiatives, fully embraced by Ham who began his military service as a private and retired as a four-star general.

For Jansen, a day does not pass without thinking about those under his command who did not make it home or otherwise suffered from their deployment to Iraq. While the grief is shared equally within the battalion, the burden weighs heaviest on the shoulders of the command.

Whether a mission was humanitarian or providing direct support to the coalition forces, the 133rd was nonetheless functioning in a war-zone environment. That dynamic in combination with the battalion's wide geographic region of responsibility necessitated that all the troops balanced multiple tasks and responsibilities, including guard and convoy duty. There were no exceptions, including Jansen and the other officers. While each day was intense and arguably so at a higher level for the battalion commander, Jansen found that it was "easy to maintain focus because there were no distractions like there are in civilian life." In an active war zone, the responsibilities and the pressure of command leadership is very much a twenty-four seven proposition.

As we closed our conversation and I was preparing to leave, John and Rae-Lynn invited me to stay for lunch. It was an easy invitation to accept, and over a delicious chicken salad with a dining room view of the lake and the mushy ice blanket that was giving way to the warming days of April, I shared the love story of Chris and Lavinia.

The conversation expanded to the challenges of loved ones who are home, going about a daily routine while a family member is thousands of miles away in a war zone. Today's advanced communication systems may ease the unknowns and help to keep people connected but they can't make the burden and stress go away. Those emotions are always close, regardless of the distance.

Note: Chapters 7 and 8 include two lengthy interviews conducted by the author with Colonel John Jansen at his home on April 6, 2019, and July 2, 2022. Additionally, the author and Jansen periodically exchanged emails over the approximate period of 2019 through July 2022. Jansen served as the battalion commander of the Maine Army National Guard 133rd Engineering Battalion during its deployment to Iraq in 2004 through 2005.

[1] Major General John W. "Bill" Libby (retired), thirty-eighth Adjutant General, Maine National Guard (2003–2012), interview with Jennifer Rooks, *Maine Watch*, a program of Maine Public Broadcasting (December 8, 2010).

[2] Eric Maddox, *Mission: Black List #1: The Inside Story of the Search for Saddam Hussein* (HarperCollins Publishers, New York, New York, 2008).

[3] W. Zach Griffith, *Packed for the Wrong Trip: A New Look Inside Abu Ghraib* (Arcade Publishing, New York, New York, 2016).

4. Justin Ellis, "Maine Troops Say Goodbye, Hit the Road," *Portland Press Herald* (January 7, 2004).
5. The Council on Foreign Relations, *The Iraq War Timeline: 2003–2011*.
6. Bill Nemitz, "Bracing for Iraq," *Maine Sunday Telegram*, February 8, 2004.
7. Wikipedia, *Geography of Mosul, Iraq*.
8. *Task Force Olympia*. Following the events of 9/11, the United States Army's First Corps (1 Corps) began providing support for Army units deployed in the *war on terrorism*. In February 2004, 1 Corps Forward Headquarters deployed to Iraq. The element called *Task Force Olympia* deployed to Mosul, Iraq, where it assumed its mission from the 101st Airborne Division to form a headquarters to exercise commands and control of all coalition and Iraqi forces in northern Iraq.

Camp Marez, Mosul, Iraq

Spc. Christopher D. Gelineau was selected as the Guidon Bearer for the Marine Army National Guard's 133rd Engineer Battalion. The Guidon Bearer is an enlisted soldier who exemplifies the highest standards of discipline, conduct, and expertise that merits the responsibility of bearing the flag which represents so much to his fellow soldiers.

CHAPTER 8

April 20, 2004: The Convoy

I WAS PLEASED TO FIND AN EMAIL FROM Lavinia when I powered up my desktop computer on Monday, April 12, 2004. In the late evening of the previous day and under the subject line, *How I've Been Lately,* Lavi shared her growing anxieties for Chris's safety in Iraq and the unanswered question of her future in the job market as graduation grew closer:

Dear Neal,

> I haven't written for a long, long time. I'm sorry but life hasn't been treating me all that nicely. I feel extremely overwhelmed by myself and trying to cope with Chris being in a dangerous place for months to come. And what's driving me crazy the most is the question as to why our soldiers are there. What are their lives put in danger for? I am still outraged and upset. Of course I support the troops, I love my soldier, but I still can't help wondering why this war is taking place to begin with. Why is my husband there for?
>
> Anyway, health wise I am doing well. I drive now so that's a big help. I am now trying

to find an internship with an advertising agency in Portland. No luck so far and the semester is almost over. I am graduating this May with two degrees: English and Business Admin + a concentration in Marketing. I feel I am reaching a dead end. I speak 4 languages, I've got 2 degrees and I am heading into a "black" hole. I know I've had better times. I just don't know how long I'll be able to go without breaking down completely. I'm holding on still.

Best always, Lavinia

In my response to Lavinia's anguished message, I acknowledged the genesis of wars as a testimony to man's egocentric inclination to resolve issues through violence, and I concluded my note with this: "You are an extremely talented woman with much to give. Never lose faith in yourself and try to stay focused on the future. Hopefully, there are brighter days ahead. Call on me if you need help or just want a friend to speak to."

Within days of my email exchange with Lavi, dramatic, on the ground reports from Mosul captured the headlines of the *Portland Press Herald* and the *Maine Sunday Telegram.* Journalist Bill Nemitz along with Photojournalist Gregory Rec were embedded with the 133rd for three weeks. Quite likely, Lavinia read every word of Nemitz's April 14, 2004, story.

Nemitz's observation that "With civil unrest all over Iraq, any trip to downtown Mosul—day or night is an exercise in extreme caution," bluntly confirmed the perception of chaos that Americans saw when they turned on the news. The experiences of soldiers like Specialist Phil Daniels of Lyman, Maine, that "You have to be on the alert for anything that's going on," reinforced the dangers of the insurgency that was dominating news from Iraq.

Lavinia probably also read Nemitz's April 18 report back to Maine. Under the alarming headline, INSIDE IRAQ: CONVOY HITS ROAD THROUGH DANGER, WEAPONS AT THE READY, GUARDSMEN HEAD OUT FROM CAMP MAREZ PAST AMBUSH ALLEY TO THE "THE

Castle," Nemitz detailed the planning specifics, safety procedures, and potential dangers facing a seventy-mile round trip convoy from Mosul to "The Castle" in the town of Tall Afar. Used as a prison by Saddam Hussein during the Iraq-Iran War, the 133rd was upgrading The Castle as a training facility for the fledgling Iraqi Army.

April 20, 2004
The Midnight Hours

With the seven-hour time difference separating Mosul from Maine, the lonely midnight hours were the most challenging for Lavi. If awake, as she often was during the darkness of early morning, her thoughts would naturally turn to Chris, who was going about his day many thousand miles away.

The highlight of each day was a Yahoo! Instant Messenger call with Chris, who had left behind a digital camera that was attached to Lavi's computer, thereby allowing them to see each other. Those sessions were tinged with the bittersweet of real-time communication between two people in love. They can see and hear each other but lack the confirming comfort of human touch. Real-time communication was reassuring, but the venue also amplified the reality of their two distinct worlds.

Just as the consequences of their lives had brought them together, the consequences of events and the decisions of powerful people separated them again. While their spirits and souls remained united, Lavi was overwhelmed with a sixth sense of doom, a premonition that the world they shared was destined to be but a memory.

Her efforts to suppress the foreboding would be eased at times from the reminders of Chris in their apartment: his civilian clothes, favorite books, music, and photos of the two of them, happy together in their young marriage. The spontaneity of their photographed smiles captured dreams of the future, but the apartment was also akin to an instant messenger session, a sweet and bitter roller coaster that would only loosen its grip when Chris finally returned to fill the void with his smile, warmth, and love.

IF YOU LOVE SOMEONE, YOU MUST TELL THEM

In the evening hours of April 19 and early morning hours of April 20, 2004, Lavi's emotions and fears were likely at fever pitch. As she lay in bed thinking of her husband in that faraway land, she must have prayed that in a few hours, a giant sigh of relief would be her reward for the extreme mental anxiety that enveloped her. It had been a countdown of hours and minutes since she learned from Chris that on April 20, he would be part of a longer convoy mission.

Since arriving in Mosul, Chris had twice traveled the five miles from Camp Freedom, one of many palatial palaces that had been used by Saddam Hussein, to FOB Marez, where most of the soldiers in the 133rd were headquartered. Chris had not been on any convoys beyond Mosul. Lavi's stress level and fears for Chris's safety were likely reinforced by the newspaper stories of the last few days detailing the dangers of a long convoy and references to shells, bunkers, weapons, and ambush alley.

Given the seven-hour differential between Maine and Mosul, Lavi's middle-of-the-night awakenings would bring her to the realization that Chris was either having breakfast or the convoy mission was underway.

If Chris was having breakfast, it would be with Specialist Greg Fiore. The two of them usually met for breakfast around 0700 hours in between the night and day shifts. And that's what they did on April 20. Fiore recalls how they talked about many things that morning and particularly about Lavi, who had told Chris in one of their recent calls that she had a "bad feeling and was freaked out" about the convoy mission. Fiore offered to take Chris's place, but the process for making such a change so close to the mission was near impossible.

Sergeant First Class (SFC) Alicia Newbegin was the operations sergeant for the headquarter command staff (HCS) at FOB Marez. Before the 133rd deployed to Iraq, Newbegin was a full-time member of the battalion, working out of the Portland Armory. Chris was part time and allowed to fulfill his guard obligation at the armory while attending the University of Southern Maine. With that regular interaction, Newbegin and Chris became good friends. In my interview with Newbegin, she shared how Chris had called her the day before the convoy, scared and anxious about the next day's mission.

Master Sergeant Greg Madore was the battalion's communication NCOIC (noncommissioned officer in charge) and assigned to the task force headquarters at the Palace. That role carried the responsibility to manage all the 133rd's communications resources, including the unique details of each convoy, summarized by Madore as "ensuring that we had the correct number of vehicles, and soldiers for the mission." He explained that efforts were "always made to combine trips to minimize multiple convoys...and other details included responsibility for generating the Convoy Clearance, requesting intelligence updates, maps, and disseminating that material to the convoy."

Understandably, longer distance convoys required even greater coordination and logistical details. To ensure that there was no favoritism for convoy assignments, Madore demonstrated exemplary leadership by personally participating in close to two convoys while also maintaining a duty roaster that tracked all convoy assignments on a rotating basis.

Convoys consisted of at least three Humvees and at least three soldiers in each vehicle. Like all tasks in the military, a DA Form 6 was completed for every mission, including the detail of personnel assigned. While assignments were made on a rotating basis, drivers, convoy commanders, and gunners were considered specialists and consequently assigned to convoy duty more frequently than others such as Chris or Specialist Jonathan Higgins.

The inherent risks that every convoy faced could never be underestimated. Charlie Company commander, Captain Michael Mitchell, left no doubt of that threat, telling journalist Nemitz, "This is the most dangerous thing we do... Nothing we do is more dangerous than this."

Convoys were carefully planned and scripted with the placement of specific vehicles and troops' seating assignments, together with radio frequencies and vehicle formations for different situations. And according to Mitchell, "Each and every mission must have a 'safety briefing, no exceptions.'"

Survival also depends on the seamless completion of protocol details critical to the success or failure of a mission. Thus, putting aside the fateful question of who was riding in the convoy and who was not, Fitch recalls that a check of the route, or "sweep the lanes" as the task was called, was supposed to be conducted by the regular Army. While efforts to confirm whether this check had been completed on April 20 were unsuccessful, it nonetheless serves as an example of the precision required up and down the chain for a successful mission. That's the skill part, but the luck part is never far away.

While many convoy missions began and ended at FOB Marez, that was not always the case. On April 20, 2004, the convoy that Chris was assigned would depart from Camp Freedom (the Palace). Madore recalls that day as if it were yesterday.

"This convoy was to support a Fire Fighting Team assigned to us. I assisted in setting up the clearance and assigning soldiers to assist as security. I sat in on the briefing the day before and listened in the morning just prior to departure. All the briefings seemed complete and correct. This was Chris' first convoy out of Mosul… He had done one or two between FOB Marez and Camp Freedom. I recall talking to Chris the night before and again that morning and he didn't want to be in the convoy. We talked about the fact that it was his turn and we all took turns."

Similar to other soldiers, the sudden change from college campus and civilian life to separation from the love of his life to the battlefields of Iraq was overwhelming to Chris. Undoubtedly, those emotions were heightened by the fact that the mission on April 20 was his first long-distance convoy.

Madore's reference to the mission of escorting a firefighting team was specific to the South Carolina 268th Engineer Firefighter Detachment that had been directed to an FOB forty miles north of Mosul. It was to be a same day, round trip. Also participating was the 204th Engineering Battalion out of New York. The convoy commander was Lieutenant Matthew Delk of the 268th, who was seated in the front passenger side of the lead vehicle, which was driven by Specialist Craig Ardry of the 133rd, from Pittsfield, Maine. Chris was seated behind Ardry. Battalion Commander Jansen had authorized the use of his assigned vehicle to serve as the lead, as it had recently been modified under the battalion's "up-armored" program.

As the four-vehicle convoy was waved through the heavily guarded security of Camp Freedom, it quickly fell into a single-file formation with vehicles separated by about 150 feet, the standard for urban travel. Once beyond the urban area and moving at a faster speed, the convoy would establish a wider separation. It was about 8:45 a.m. in Iraq and 1:45 a.m. back in Maine as one of Saddam Hussein's former palatial palaces receded in to the background.

According to Higgins, the convoy headed south on what the soldiers referred to as MSR Tampa (Iraq Route 1), which goes through the west side of Mosul. While the trip was to take about one hour, Higgins recalls hearing that the convoy was delayed in traffic for a few minutes. As emphasized time and again by Captain Mitchell, the soldiers in the convoy sat alertly in their seats, bullets loaded in their M16s, safety switches on but with fingers on the safeties.

Driving the second vehicle of the convoy was Specialist Sok San Pao, a former track star and graduate of Portland's Deering High School. Pao had joined the Maine National Guard shortly before 9/11 and realized that the attack on America would likely involve him. Pao's story as reported by Joshua Weinstein of the *Portland Press Herald* is inspiring and represents the ideal of America when refugees who have run out of options find a welcome mat on our shores. His dad was a professor in Cambodia who fled that country when another dictator, Pol Pot, came to power. Like so many dictators, Pol Pot did not trust freethinking intellectuals and would often go to the extreme of murder to silence them. Born in a refugee camp in Thailand, Pao and his entire family found a home in Maine in 1985.

Years later when I met Pao for lunch, he described the April 20 convoy that he was a part of and admitted that he was unable to discuss it for many years. The four Humvees had been exiting Mosul for about ten minutes and traveling on a divided highway. Pao "sensed something was coming," as they neared an exit ramp, and he suddenly realized that there were no people to be seen in the busy neighborhood. No people to be seen in a busy neighborhood spelled potential trouble, the very formula U.S. forces had been warned to be aware of.

While describing himself as "not particularly religious," in the instant that Pao was processing the setting, he prayed two times to the Buddha in his pocket that his grandmother gave him when he left for Iraq. And in that moment, the thunderous blast of an IED (improvised explosive device) in the median strip hurled the lead vehicle into a "twisted, burning, contortion of steel and shattered glass." Pao's vehicle, directly behind the lead vehicle, and the other two vehicles in the convoy were jolted and damaged but not destroyed. In keeping with protocol, Pao cleared the scene and proceeded a short distance to a more secure site. Within seconds, rapid gunfire rained down from abutting buildings that were providing cover for an estimated dozen insurgents.

Back at Camp Freedom, Higgins remembers hearing and feeling the tremors of the blast and seeing the smoke from their office window. The impact of the blast on the convoy GPS made it hard to establish accurate grid locations to guide the medevac. As one of the two battalion, Intel Analysts, with expertise in mapping and geospatial technology, Higgins was able to assist the medevac crew in establishing the location of the attack.

The ensuing firefight was brief with the U.S. soldiers returning fire and injuring or killing four of the insurgents. Pao reacted swiftly and was able to clear the scene and identify a nearby area from which to radio for medevac and backup support. Not knowing the full status of the situation, Pao returned to the scene, where he found the other soldiers providing aid to the injured as medical helicopters arrived followed by reinforcements from the Second Infantry Division's Stryker Brigade.

While medically alive, Chris was unconscious from the moment of the blast. He and Specialist Craig Ardry were airlifted to a nearby military hospital at Camp Diamondback, where they were met by Major Dwaine Drummond, executive officer of the 133rd.

Drummond, who is now a brigadier general, recalls how he held Chris's hand and spoke to him, even though he knew Chris was unconscious. Along with Command Sergeant Major (CSM) David

Wilkinson of Standish, Maine, Drummond remained with Chris during the subsequent flight to Baghdad. On that flight, the twenty-three-year-old soldier from Vermont became the 133rd's first combat casualty since World War II.

Years later when I interviewed, Staff Sergeant Hal Fitch and Specialist Jonathan Higgins each believed or had reason to believe that they and not Chris were supposed to be riding in the convoy on the twentieth. Along with Fiore, over the years since Iraq, all three have confronted feelings of "survivor guilt."

Through my conversations with Battalion Commander Jansen and Master Sergeant Greg Madore, I reaffirmed to Fitch, Higgins, and Fiore that the decision to assign Chris was consistent with the battalion's policies and that it was Chris's turn to be on a longer convoy mission. In a December 31, 2004, *Boston Globe* interview, Lavi told the reporter she had "felt it coming…that she woke up twice during the night, panicked."

No matter how it's parsed, these are the tragic "what ifs" of life, accentuated tenfold in war. Not found in the data, the realities of war haunt survivors and loved ones for the rest of their lives. Over the time that Fiore, Higgins, and Fitch spent in Iraq, they all rode on many convoys. And according to Fitch, there were a number of "close calls," usually including mortar rounds, together with constant threats and protests. Fitch rode in over sixty convoys, occasionally as the convoy commander. "The first few were very nerve racking," he told me, "but with more under my belt, it felt like waking up and going to do my job in the morning." Fitch remembers wishing Chris, "Good luck and God bless on your safe return." As Higgins succinctly summarized, "No one wanted to be on convoys."

Lieutenant Christopher Elgee (now lieutenant colonel), who had been at Camp Freedom communicating directly with the convoy, would later praise Delk, saying, "He was quite the hero from what I heard in pulling Gelineau and Ardry from the burning vehicle… I have no doubt that he saved Ardry's life." Ardry's injuries were extensive and extremely serious. According to a news report in the May 29, 2007, edition, Reporter Sharon Kiley Mack of the *Bangor Daily News*, Ardry, "suffered a shattered leg, broken knee cap, a paralyzed vocal cord, fractured pelvis, broken ribs, burns to both hands, shrapnel in his face, a shattered eardrum and a concussion. In the immediate days that followed he died twice and was resuscitated and remained unconscious for eleven days." In that same article, Ardry shares the very human response to second-guess, saying, "I sometimes blame myself: Could I have been driving slower? Faster?"

Others from the 133rd who were injured included Pao with smoke inhalation, neck and back pain, and Specialist Dwight Nickles, who suffered a perforated eardrum. Injured from the 268th were Lieutenant Mathew Delk, with burns to the face and second-degree burns on both hands and Staff Sergeant (SGT) Charles Boone, who suffered from a concussion and post-traumatic stress disorder. Specialist Herson Gutierrez of the 204th also suffered a concussion and injury to his knee.

Regrouping

Shortly after the attack, there was an immediate need for the leaders of the 133rd to regroup, assess what had happened, clarify next steps, and establish the process for moving forward. Absent a unified message, a swirl of misinformation and rumors would only further exacerbate the tragedy. Accordingly, all outside communications, Internet, and telephone were suspended to ensure that details of the attack were internally understood, that lines of communication with the soldiers were clearly in place, and that appropriate notifications were conducted prior to a formal announcement to the media.

Among the early notifications, Battalion Commander Jansen informed Maine Governor John Baldacci before news leaked out. Jansen had to go to the roof of one of the buildings at Camp Freedom to ensure there was a strong signal for the call.

Jansen would later say, "What the soldiers did on that site was absolutely amazing. They not only engaged the threat, they got everybody out…to a place where they could start the MEDEVAC procedures right away." While Jansen's vehicle was badly damaged, the fact that it had recently been "up armored" may have saved Delk and Ardry's lives.

As if the attack itself was not enough, Jansen was meeting that day with a media contingent who had scheduled time with him for a *Project Overview of Task Force Olympia*. Because details of the attack were being learned in parallel with the media meetings, a careful balancing act was required to ensure that word of the attack was not prematurely released to the media.

At that time, John W. "Bill" Libby was adjutant general of the Maine National Guard, appointed to that highest position by Governor John Baldacci. Given his position, Libby was one of the very first to learn of the attack and Chris's death. Years later, Libby and I emailed back and forth, and when he returned to Maine from his winter home in Florida, we got together over a pizza and beer at Sebago Brewing Company in Gorham, Maine. Reflecting back on April 20, 2004, he recalled how a Maine National Guard fixed-wing aircraft was dispatched to meet him in North Carolina on the twenty-first to return him to Augusta in order to begin the planning for Chris's return and funeral.

In that same interview, Libby went on to share, "After spending 10 years on Active Duty in the Army, including a tour in Vietnam, I was not unfamiliar with deaths in combat. We lost dozens of soldiers in my Battalion in Vietnam during the year I was in that country, and, during my three years as an ROTC instructor at UMASS Amherst. I had to make numerous Notifications to Next of Kin [NOK], of the deaths of loved ones in Vietnam."

Despite his experience in Vietnam, Libby added, "I found myself on new ground dealing with the death of a soldier whose unit I had 'sent' to Iraq. I did not pick them to go to Iraq, the National Guard Bureau did based on the needs in the theater, but I did sign the orders. I've always said it was easier to go myself than send others and still carry that thought."

Because Chris's death was the first combat casualty involving a Maine National Guard soldier since World War II, Libby arrived to find the staff reviewing the protocols and planning Chris's funeral. Those included the designation of Chief Warrant Officer 4 Cliff Small to serve as the casualty notification officer for Lavinia, and for the father, it was Brigadier General Shailor from Vermont National Guard since Chris's dad lived in Vermont.

Back in Maine

By early evening of April 20 in Iraq, late morning / early afternoon in Maine, communications for the 133rd were restored and news of an incident leaked to the outside world. More specific news was communicated back to the MENG headquarters in Augusta detailing the injured and the death of Chris. The sequence of events suggests that at about the time Chris was being airlifted to Baghdad, Lavinia was probably getting ready for the day, nervously anticipating that she would hear from Chris later in the day.

When the 133rd deployed, the Maine National Guard Family Readiness Program formed a family support group. The program was coordinated by Staff Sergeant Barbara Claudell in the Augusta command center. In the Portland area, group sessions were held at the Maine National Guard Armory on Stevens Avenue in Portland. Families were encouraged to find a special "battle buddy" with whom they could mutually lean on, confide to, and always be there for each other.

One of the active leaders of the support group was Linda Newbegin of Standish, Maine. Linda's husband, Wayne, had served in the MENG for thirty-nine years, rising to the position of operations sergeant for the state before retiring as a master sergeant in 1999. Their daughter, Sergeant First Class Alicia Newbegin, and her husband, Command Sergeant Major David Wilkinson, were serving together in Mosul with the 133rd, while their two young children were cared for by Alicia's sister and her husband who lived next door to Linda and Wayne.

In one of my interviews with Linda Newbegin, she recalled the first time she met Lavinia. The occasion was a family briefing shortly after the announcement that the 133rd would deploy to Iraq. Although Chris and Lavi were sitting in the back of the room, Newbegin noticed the intensity of Lavi's focus. At the end of the program, Lavi made a beeline to Newbegin and peppered her with a string of questions in search of assurance that all would be okay. While there were no guarantees, Newbegin offered her sincere empathy, reinforced by the fact that her daughter and son-in-law would also be heading to Iraq.

After the 133rd arrived in Iraq, Newbegin encouraged Lavi to attend a group support session. While Lavi had established contact with a few other spouses and continued to reach out to family and friends, she had not participated in any of those sessions. Recently, however, Lavi had told Newbegin that she would probably attend the next meeting of the group, scheduled coincidentally for the evening of April 20.

In the afternoon of April 20, knowing that Newbegin had stayed in touch with Lavi since deployment of the 133rd, Claudell called Newbegin to inform that Chris had been killed. She explained that efforts to locate Lavi had been unsuccessful, and therefore, Newbegin should plan on arriving at the meeting early, in the event that Lavi showed up.

It would later be rumored but never confirmed that Lavi had spent much of the day at the USM Library. Aware that Chris was on a long convoy mission but not knowing when he would return to Mosul undoubtedly heightened Lavi's anxiety. Next to her love for being with Chris, libraries had always offered a calming refuge where she was at peace with herself and the special love she held for books and learning. While speculative, it seems quite likely that Lavi's path on that tragic day would have led to the library.

Feeling the weight of the sad news she held, Newbegin made a point to arrive early to the support group meeting. She remembers vividly the events of that night. "Chaplain Gibson and CW4 Small arrived at the Stevens Avenue Armory about 30 minutes before the support meeting was to start. I walked downstairs and saw them come in the building in their dress uniforms…not a good sign. I immediately rushed them down a side hall on the first floor, our support meeting was on the 2nd. I went back to the 2nd floor and sat by the door. Lavi arrived about a half hour late. I rushed her to the other side of the building where the Chaplain and CW4 Small were, telling her I had something for her. She immediately knew something was wrong and began sobbing."

As reported by Barbara Walsh of the *Portland Press Herald*, two "battle buddies," Kim Kelley and Judy Dix, were at the family support group meeting. Kelley said that Lavi "left the room and then we heard the screams…the hairs on my neck stood up." Upon learning that the woman who left the room was the wife of the soldier who had been killed, Kelley and Dix "held each other," and Kelley was so shaken that she collapsed on the stairs when leaving the building. "My legs just gave out on me," she said.

Lavi would later describe in an audio interview how she remembered "Chaplain Gibson saying, 'Mrs. Gelineau, I regret to inform you…' That's all I remember. I literally felt my chest crack and couldn't feel my legs."

The audio interview, *The Cost of War*, was recorded by S. Spencer Scott for the *Blunt Youth Radio Project*, a program of the University of Southern Maine radio station, WMPG. At the time of the interview, Scott was a senior in high school, and in my conversation with him, he remembered Lavi as "very focused, and reflective."[1]

Newbegin said Lavi was understandably inconsolable, and at one point, Small called for MED-Q, the City of Portland's emergency medical service, to assist in assessing her condition. So distraught was Lavi that Chaplain Gibson called in Robin Walsh, the leader of the 133rd Bravo Company support group. Robin quickly came to the armory. She and Newbegin brought Lavi back to her apartment and remained with her through the night.

During the long hours of that night and between her anguished sobs, Lavi spoke of the depth of love that she and Chris shared, how smart he was, and his "beautiful face." She lay down for a while and spoke with Chris's dad, John Gelineau, back in Vermont. In the morning at Lavi's request, Newbegin called Father Sarantides of the Greek Orthodox Church, who came to the apartment to offer prayers, counsel, and support.

Gelineau received the news of his son's death on the night of April 20 and early the next morning, drove from Vermont to Lavinia and Chris's apartment in Portland. Arriving around 10:30 a.m., he found his daughter-in-law devastated, her "American dream" crushed. "Her purpose in life had been taken away, in that moment, when she was told that Chris was dead," Gelineau said. Her cries of "What am I going to do now?" greeted Gelineau and continued as he struggled with the devastating loss of his son. Over those first few days, Lavi came to realize that the answer was not to silently accept what had happened. That would be affirmation of a war that made no sense to her and to millions of others.

The next day, April 21, 2004, Maine governor, John Baldacci, pursuant to his authority as commander in chief of the Maine National Guard, announced the names of the soldiers injured or killed in the attack. The governor called the families of all four Guard members. Of Chris, Baldacci said, "Specialist Gelineau paid the highest price for the freedoms we cherish in this country. He showed great strength of character, not only in his work in Iraq, but throughout his life. He was committed to his family, his state, and his nation." Baldacci went on to praise the 133rd and announce that the flag would be flown at half-staff on the day of Chris's funeral.[2]

A punch to the gut

The news of Chris's death was greeted with disbelief and shock. It most certainly hit me that way, a gut punch like no other. It just wasn't supposed to happen. Chris had barely arrived in Iraq. It was his first long convoy. He and his bride had been featured in the send-off of the 133rd. He was too young, too full of life and love, and carried a wonderful boyish smile that deserved to be shared for decades yet to come—a description that fits millions who have died in wars.

My reaction of shock and disbelief was the same as the others in the office who had come to know Lavi and like me, had met Chris. That special smile was burned into my memory in a place where it doesn't fade. And as I had suggested, the day after meeting Chris, his résumé was sitting on my desk. While it had been a while since Lavi's internship ended, our "corporate culture" at the council of governments fostered continuing contact with many "alums" and to be supportive in both bad and good times.

That spirit was an unwritten guiding principle, but as in many organizations, there is usually one who simply takes care of any and all kinds of details. Maddy Adams was that person. Maddy wasn't just my right hand. She was everybody's, kind of like Chris who would see something that needed to be done and simply do it. Within a day of the public announcement of Chris's death, Maddy sent a note to our staff, reminding us of the connection between Chris and Lavinia, whom she described as "a sweet, bubbly girl…very much in love with her husband Chris…and with her family in Romania we are concerned for her welfare…some of us are planning on pitching in some money to send to Lavinia because she never had much…if you want to help, please see me."

In my response to Maddy's initiative and to the staff, I described the "tragic, heavy loss that leaves me with a heavy heart" and how I had reached out to Chris's dad to express our deepest condolences. I also shared with the staff how Lavi had very recently sent an email to me expressing her "increasing fear for Chris's safety." And I closed my message with the hope that a scholarship fund or other fitting memorial might be established.

Back in Vermont on the next day, Chris's best friends from high school, Travis and Leslie Scribner, were going about their busy day as usual. Leslie was the first to hear via a phone call from Lavi. At first, all she could hear was sobbing. Finally, she heard Lavi's voice, "Chris is dead. My baby's gone." Leslie, trying to grasp what she heard, tried to converse, but Lavi hung up. Leslie knew that Chris was in Iraq, but it was impossible to filter what she heard. Her thoughts quickly went to her husband, Travis, knowing that he would be devastated. He and Chris were best friends, each best man for the other, and when Chris was the new kid in school, it was Travis who took him under his wing like a big brother.

Gathering her thoughts and composure as best she could, Leslie called Travis on his cell phone and asked when he would be home. Travis explained that he still had a couple of stops to make. She pressed him further, and he asked what it was all about. Realizing that he would not be satisfied until she told him why it was important to come home now, Leslie said, "Okay, but you need to pull over." Travis was devastated, "wailing" into the phone and blindsided in disbelief.

Word spread quickly within their circle of friends. While the years since high school were few, the crushing news of a classmate killed in a faraway war, coming within three years of 9/11, was another grim reminder of how life catches up to all of us. Chris's friends did what others throughout time have done when faced with a numbing tragedy. They came together that night in order to be together at the home of Travis and Leslie. Shared grief helps to stay connected to life. It's cathartic. They would later organize a memorial service in Burlington for family, friends, teachers, and members of the Vermont National Guard.

At about that same time and miles away in Maine, a similar scene played out. Lavi's favorite professor and confidante, Margaret Reimer, who understood the personal side of war from her youth when her father served in Vietnam, collected her thoughts and composed a letter to Michael Moore who was compiling, *Will They Ever Trust Us Again? Letters from the War Zone*. Explaining that both Chris and Lavinia were former students of hers, Reimer wrote how she had just heard of Chris's death.

"I was on my way home when Maine Public Radio announced the name of the soldier who died. I had to pull over onto a side road in Webbs Mill [believe me it's all side roads out there] so that I could phone my husband and vent my grief and rage. Besides, it's not safe to drive while sobbing. I don't want it to seem that I believe Christopher Gelineau was any more valuable than any of the other six hundred soldiers who have died in Iraq to date, or more valuable than the thousands of Iraqis who are dying every day. However, I knew him and I know his wife, Lavinia, and I cannot bear to think of the burden of grief that she now must carry." Reimer went on to share how close she was to Lavinia and more so since Chris's deployment. She closed her letter with a touching sentiment, "Death in Iraq has a face—it's a sweet, young face, smiling adoringly toward the beautiful bride on his arm. Chris was 23. Lavinia is too young to be a widow."[3]

IF YOU LOVE SOMEONE, YOU MUST TELL THEM

The death of Specialist Christopher Gelineau of the Maine Army National Guard was big news in the print and electronic media of Maine and Vermont and further amplified in the *Boston Globe* and over the *New England Cable News Network*.

As April 20, 2004, came to a close, the "bad feelings" that Chris and Lavinia had shared about the pending convoy were now a chapter in the multiple volumes of the tragic history of multiple wars. Chris's last meal, his breakfast with Specialist Fiore, was memorialized eight years later on *The Fallen Heroes of Operation Iraqi Freedom* website.

"Its been 8 years today Chris. I still remember sitting with you at breakfast that morning. You told me that both you and your wife had a bad feeling about the convoy. Wish I went in your place."

Greg F. of Naples, Maine

The 133rd Says Goodbye

Friday, April 24, 2004
1000 hours

The day was typical for Iraq's Nineveh province in late April, temps in the seventies to eighties with a dry stillness hanging over the Tigris River Valley, punctuating the horizon with a look and feel of the ancient images associated with that part of the world.

Specialist Christopher D. Gelineau arrived in Mosul, Iraq, in February 2004. Two months later, the soldiers of the Maine Army National Guard 133rd Engineering Battalion came together at FOB Marez to honor Chris, their friend and fellow soldier, with prayers, song, words, and tears. Presided over by the battalion chaplain, Captain David Sivret of Calais, Maine, participants included Major Dwaine Drummond (executive officer of the 133rd), who read a message from Governor Baldacci, Captain Michael Steinbuchel (commander of the 133rd's Headquarters Support Company, the unit to which Chris was assigned), and the battalion commander, Lieutenant Colonel John Jansen.

Jansen's remarks were moving and emotional. "There are very few days in my life that I can define as life changing, April 20th, 2004, was one of these days and I know that on that day I changed forever." Describing Chris as "special with a way of making difficult days a little brighter," Jansen cited his "contagious smile, quick wit and humor" and shared that he joined the National Guard in order to have the opportunity to go to college. He went to say that although "Chris did not support the war and was torn to leave the love of his life, he accepted his responsibilities as a soldier and deployed with the 133rd Engineering Battalion for Iraq."[4]

Jansen interacted with Chris on a daily basis and that one of the responsibilities Chris was particularly proud of was his selection as the battalion guidon bearer for the 133rd. "Guidon Bearer is an enlisted soldier who exemplifies the highest standards of discipline, conduct and expertise that merits the responsibility of bearing the flag which represents so much to his fellow soldiers."

In a letter to Lavinia Gelineau, Jansen wrote, "I will never forget the day when he carried our colors during a formal acceptance of authority ceremony for the mission here in Iraq. He stood tall with a smile on his face and I could tell that he was very proud to be the one carrying our flag and streamers representing those have served before us. We made the right choice when we selected Chris, and for me he will forever remain the unit's Guidon Bearer."[5]

Services for military and civilian public safety personnel often include a *last roll call* followed by the sounding of taps. When experienced, there is nothing more emotional and reaffirming of the purpose and risk of service. *Portland Press Herald* reporter Bill Nemitz described the *last roll call* at Chris's service:

> First Sergeant (1SG) Thomas Conroy strode to the podium and, in words much louder than any yet spoken, ordered, "Attention to roll call!"
>
> The battalion rose as one and stood at attention.
>
> "Bucklin!" called Conroy.
>
> "Here, 1st sergeant!" hollered Staff Sergeant Richard Bucklin.
>
> "Chadwick!"

"Here, 1st sergeant!" responded Staff Sergeant Mark Chadwick.

"Dix!"

"Here, 1st sergeant!" bellowed Sergeant First Class Chuck Dix.

"Gelineau!" shouted Conroy.

Silence. Conroy took a deep breath.

"Gelineau!"

Only silence.

With that, the first mournful notes of taps filled the hall. Up and down the long rows, soldiers lowered their heads and wept.

Maine remembers

On the first day of May 2004, eleven days after Chris died, family, friends, the USM community, members of the military, and others who had never met Chris Gelineau came together at the University of Southern Maine campus in Portland to pay tribute to the young American soldier.

A few months earlier, that young soldier was an American college student, cruising down the home stretch to graduation, embraced by the love of his life, and brimming with the confidence that a challenging career and full life awaited him. The university had been the happy place for Chris and Lavi—where their lives intersected, where they fell in love, and where their most special moments were shared.

It was a warm, sunny Saturday, one of those days in northern New England where it finally feels that winter has passed. The last remnants of dirty snow have melted, and newly forming leaves sporting the virgin green of their optimistic tender age are decorating the drab, gray limbs of winter.

As I entered the USM gym, a sea of faces covered every square foot on the basketball court. I settled into one of the remaining bleacher seats, and from my high perch, I watched Lavinia and her family, all of whom I had met the previous day at the funeral home, as they entered along with Chris's family. The crowd was somber and quiet as the flag-draped coffin was slowly rolled in by a six-soldier honor guard.

The memorial service was a carefully planned blend of military protocol, prayers of remembrance and love, and sharing of memories and tributes to Chris. Speakers included Chris's mother, Victoria Chicoine, and his uncle, John Chicoine. Condolences were extended by Maine's two senators, Olympia Snowe and Susan Collins. Governor Baldacci presented Lavinia with the State of Maine flag that had flown over the state capitol.

Maine National Guard Chaplain Andy Gibson recognized Chris for the high standards he set for himself and the 133rd and shared how Chris had independently initiated an effort to improve the efficiency of convoys through a review and analysis of logistical data. That was Chris. He was of the stripe that didn't have to be told what to do. If he saw a need, his automatic response was to figure out a way to make it better.

Father Sarantides of the Greek Orthodox Church in Portland spoke in a measured, reassuring voice, recalling how, "Christopher had come with his wife, Lavinia, just before leaving for deployment, and he asked for prayers. I prayed for his safety and honorable service, and I could tell just how moved he was by the prayers. And I prayed for his wife, who would be waiting and praying for him day and night. They were so much in love. It was the last time I would see him alive."

Echoing Lavi's own sentiment, Father Sarantides added, "The value of a life is not measured by number of years lived. One can live twenty-three years and still accomplish more than someone who lives eighty years. The quality of life is measured not by length of years but selfless service. And by this measure, how fully Christopher Gelineau lived! His face spoke of kindness. His eyes seemed to be always focused on someone else—most often on his beloved wife, to be sure—but everyone who knew him spoke of his eagerness to help serve his country and the needs of others. What a beautiful witness to the love of God that animated his heart and soul."

Kevin Wack, a staff writer for the *Portland Press Herald*, wrote that "among many sad moments at Saturday's memorial service...

nothing was more touching than the composed grace and eloquence of the wife who loved him." First directing her comments to the crowd, Lavi shared how she and Chris were hopeless lovers, kissing before and after every class. Then directing her comments to her husband, Lavi said, "You showed me what perfect love was when other people could not even dream of true love... I used to call you my sweet American pie. You used to call me your sweet Romanian chocolate... I traveled half the world to meet you, and I found you... You must be carrying me now because my heart is very light."

Reaching deep to her inner core for the strength that defined her character, Lavi found the needed chords on her guitar to sing "Right Here Waiting" by Richard Marx. At the close of her song to Chris, Lavi draped her body across the casket. You could almost hear the tears of the many fall to the floor.

With full military honors, Sergeant Christopher Gelineau was laid to rest in Portland's historic Evergreen Cemetery. I chose to not attend the burial.

Note: The following media reports are referenced in this chapter with appropriate attribution(s), embedded in the narrative.

Bill Nemitz, "Making Home in a War Zone," *Portland Press Herald* (April 14, 2004).

Bill Nemitz, "Convoy Hits Road through Danger," *Maine Sunday Telegram* (April 18, 2004).

Bill Nemitz, "Maine Soldier Dies in ambush," *Portland Press Herald* (April 21, 2004).

Joshua Weinstein, "Soldier's Family so Scared," *Portland Press Herald* (April 21, 2004).

Barbara Walsh, "Battle Buddies," *Portland Press Herald* (April).

John Richardson, "Future Held Promise for Slain Soldier," *Portland Press Herald* (April 22, 2004).

Bill Nemitz, "133rd Embraces Hero as One of Its Own," *Portland Press Herald* (April 24, 2004).

Bill Nemitz, "Tearful Service Honors Mainer," *Portland Press Herald* (April 25, 2004).

Bill Nemitz, "Trip to a Safe Haven," *Portland Press Herald* (April 28, 2004).

Sharon Kiley Mack, "Pittsfield Man Bears Wounds of War," *Bangor Daily*

IF YOU LOVE SOMEONE, YOU MUST TELL THEM

News (May 29, 2007).

Kevin Wack, *Portland Press Herald* (May 1, 2004).

Author interviews and emails regarding details of the April 20, 2004, convoy with the following: John W. Libby, John Jansen, Greg Fiore, Harold Fitch, Jonathan Higgins, Greg Madore, Michael Mitchell, Alicia Newbegin, Sok San Pao, Dwain Drummond, Christopher Elgee, Leslie Scribner, Margaret Reimer, and John Gelineau.

Lavinia Gelineau with S. Scott Spencer, "Cost of War," *Blunt Youth Radio Project*.

Notes

[1] S. Scott Spencer, audio interview with Lavinia Gelineau, "Cost of War," *WMPG: Blunt Youth Radio Project* (January 1, 2005).
[2] John E. Baldacci, *Media Advisory: Governor Pays Tribute to Maine's 133rd* (April 21, 2004).
[3] Michael Moore, "Death in Iraq Has a Face," *Will They Ever Trust Us Again?* (Margaret Reimer, p. 147).
[4] John J. Jansen remarks, memorial ceremony, Specialist Christopher Gelineau (FOB Marez, Mosul, Iraq, April 24, 2004).
[5] John J. Jansen, lieutenant colonel, engineer commanding, *Guidon Bearer Letter to Mrs. Gelineau* (April 21, 2004).

Chapter 9

Commencement

By definition, a *commencement* is a beginning. Traditionally, it is also a time of celebration. But for Lavi and her family, the occasion of the University of Southern Maine's 2004 commencement was bittersweet, as it had been just one month since Chris passed away. There was great pride, though, in recognizing that Lavinia Gelineau was graduating *magna cum laude* with a double major in English and business administration. Her late husband, Christopher D. Gelineau, who had majored in information technology communications with a minor in management information systems, was awarded his diploma posthumously. In an email to me, Lavi's best friend, Denitza Dimitrova, captured the emotions of that day:

> As the graduates began their procession into the auditorium, Iulia, John and I watched for Lavi, and, seeing her was a proud moment. Following the usual speeches by dignitaries, diplomas were presented to the graduates. When the English majors were called up, Lavi was among them, and proudly received her degree with honors.
>
> Later in the ceremony, the Information Technology graduates came forward to receive their diplomas. Lavi moved forward again, to the

stage, this time to receive the diploma for Chris that was being presented posthumously. As she approached the stage, the applause for Chris turned to a full standing ovation with a defining roar of intensity, and, only concluded when Lavi settled back in to her seat. Members of the USM staff later remarked that they had never seen anything of this scale and dimension. Chris was well liked by his classmates, and they and the rest of the audience showed their appreciation to the person he was... It was all very moving.[1]

Best of friends as Lavi and Denitza were, it was all the more special and appropriate for the two of them to be receiving their diplomas on the same day.

In the days and weeks that followed Chris's death and the USM commencement, Lavi would continue to speak out against the war. She was tormented by the irrationality of the war in Iraq and the morality of soldiers and innocent civilians serving as the pawns of the power brokers. Her emails cried out despair and when viewed collectively, are the electronic equivalent to the handwritten diaries in other times, diaries that chronicled similar tragedies and emotions of past wars and the lasting impacts on past generations. In Lavi's writings, she shared her grief and frustration with friends and others in a process that likely provided some cathartic and calming medicine of the soul.

Although a vocal critic of the war, Lavi was at heart, a giving woman with enormous empathy and love for others regardless of their opinion of the war. Those who were critical of her voice in speaking truth to power were judging her without knowing that within days of Chris's death, she was also reaching out to the soldiers and families with deeply personal touches of loving support and compassion, many of whom were also grieving or dealing with the all-consuming knot of anxiety that grips loved ones separated by war. Countless hours were spent packaging gifts to the troops in Iraq and giving her time to personally visit and call families. Soon after Chris died, Lavi was also volunteering at the Center for Grieving Children in Portland. And on those occasions in which her natural creative talents summoned her, she responded through poems and prayers.

A decision to teach

Eight months after the death of her husband, Lavi looked in the mirror and asked, "Where is your life going, girl? Who are you?" Emotionally drained, she was nonetheless moving forward with her decision to pursue a career in teaching. With the decision to dedicate her lifework to education, Lavi completed the application for admission to the Extended Teacher Education Program (ETEP). A critical component of the application was the essay.

Lavi's decision to teach followed her consideration of a career in advertising. That was one reason why she had decided on also earning a degree in business. Her look-in-the-mirror conversation is captured in the following from her ETEP essay:

> I sat down and, among others, I tried to pinpoint what I felt like doing for a living. Not what I thought I wanted to do, but what I thought I could do from the heart. I tried to picture myself working an advertising job, staring at a monitor for hours on end; spending most of the day for the rest of my life in a perfectly square cubicle, crunching numbers so I can figure out how to more efficiently and effectively sell some insignificant, useless, yet desirable, product to my target market; having a reasonable, well deserved paycheck at the end of every month as my only reward. I cringed!! That was not my calling and for sure, that could not have been what I could do best. Therefore, I dug deeper, far deeper than April 20th.

When Lavi sent me her essay, I recall how moved I was in thinking of the road she had traveled and the positive path she was now blazing. Her destiny would be in a classroom, close to a library, the holder of a doctorate degree and teaching languages at the university level. That was her goal and the passion behind her fluency of French, Spanish, English, and her native language, Romanian.

In defining the contrasting approaches to teaching as cited in her ETEP essay, it seems quite likely that Lavi came to realize that how one chose to teach should be a personal decision similar to parental choices on raising children. While there is no evidence that she consciously made a direct comparison, it would be consistent with a passage in her essay in which she wrote, "My high school English and French teachers were like parents to me. I looked forward to every one of their classes and always did my homework religiously." This, in contrast to her high school history teacher, "who made us learn instead of helping and motivating us to learn."

Lavi shared her philosophy of teaching, writing, "Teaching is not a monologue but a dialogue…therefore the role of the educator is not merely to disseminate information but to share it with students."

In drawing these distinctions, Lavi nonetheless attributed both classroom experiences as important in the development of what she projected would be her own teaching style with its emphasis on *sharing information through dialogue as opposed to monologue*. That acknowledgment speaks to a philosophy of teaching that mirrors how Lavi conducted her life and the values that guided her for a life of learning experienced through those teachers who opened her eyes to the possibility of a career in education.

The following verbatim section of her ETEP essay reflects her keen intellect and passion to teach creatively.

> Another educator who made a long-lasting impression on me and who became my role model was my ENG 262 (Poetry, The Genre) and ENG 399 (Syntax, Rhetoric, and Style) professor at USM. Most students who had her

as an instructor characterized her as "tough but fair." I thought she was brilliant and moreover, passionate and creative about her teaching. She knew how to make any difficult text appeal to us. For instance, the medieval English in Irish and Scottish ballads we had to read and interpret was extremely hard to understand. Therefore, in order to illustrate the sensibility and richness of the text, she played tapes with songs that had those same ballads for lyrics. Not only did the music capture our attention but it also conveyed, in a much simpler way, the range of emotions present in the written versions of the ballads. There was no way anyone would become bored in her class. Even those who had to be there in order to fulfill a requirement ended up participating in the class discussion and liking the class.

For Lavinia being a good teacher was the same as being a good citizen, regardless of possible differences of opinion. In proudly becoming an American citizen, Lavi was practicing what she had learned, and even with the loss of Chris, she was committed to living her life in a country that was built on the fundamental rights of free speech. Recognizing that there is far more that binds than divides us, the teacher in her understood the power for good that comes from sharing and listening to the ideas of others.

Her decision to pursue a career in education was also inspired by the words of Chris as reflected in the closing paragraph of her ETEP essay:

> Chris never compromised when it came to his dreams, to what he could do best and people looked up to him. He taught me to be true to myself and never give up; to find out what I can do best. I now know that is teaching. Before he left for Iraq, he had me promise that, should the

worst happen, I would go on for him, for me, for what we had built together. That is what I am going to do, because *where there's a dream, there's hope; where there's hope there might be a future.*

---

[1] Denitza Dimitrova, email to author (February 23, 2019).

Chapter 10

If You Love Someone, You Must Tell Them

> We would stay awake nights, and so many times we kept wondering: Oh, my goodness, we are so lucky. People live a lifetime of 90 years, and never get to meet their half. What is the chance? A girl comes from Romania to Maine, and a boy from Vermont comes to Maine, and what is the probability they go to the same school and they get to meet and complete each other?
>
> —Lavinia E. Gelineau, in tribute to her late husband, Christopher D. Gelineau

THE TWELVE MONTHS BETWEEN APRIL 2004 AND April 2005 tested Lavinia Gelineau's soul and spirit in ways that would cause many to crumble and give up. The fog of despair that had smothered Lavi since Chris and the 133rd deployed to Iraq began to lift ever so slightly to the wider horizon of her dreams.

With the bittersweet awakening that life goes on, Lavi found the peace of mind to prepare for the baby that she and Chris had planned in the event that he never made it home. I remember her telling me of the plan they made and how she was prepared to soon make it happen. It was yet one more affirmation of their love for each other and life itself.

Lavi's transition to her changed life was eased by the decision of her mother, Iulia, to remain with her in America rather than returning to Romania after Chris died. The practical financial side was also eased with the insurance money from Chris's estate. Those funds were used to purchase a house in Westbrook, Maine, a city bordering Portland. The peaceful middle-class neighborhood offered a setting of stability and opportunity for Lavi and her mother to move forward in creating a home for their new lives together.

Turning her attention to the question of a career, Lavi's keen intellectual curiosity and love of literature and languages awakened her to a calling in education as a teacher. The latent building blocks of a life with purpose, unselfish giving, and genuine love for others surfaced anew. Breaking through the tangled turmoil of grief, bitterness, and media attention, Lavi was emerging as a strong, self-confident woman, grateful to be a citizen of the United States of America. With strongly held beliefs and of independent spirit, the openness of American democracy, warts and all, offered a beacon of enlightenment that was new and exciting to her.

As a young woman from Romania, Lavinia Onitiu had traveled thousands of miles to Portland, Maine, where the consequences of her journey intersected with the consequences of the journey that brought Christopher Gelineau from Bristol, Vermont, to Portland. The common denominator of those journeys was the University of Southern Maine and the seemingly inconsequential decision of each to work one summer in the university's maintenance department.

When speaking to family and friends and sharing poetry, we see the narrative footprints of a brilliant young woman who aspired to a higher calling and inspired others along the way. A woman of enormous talent, compassion, and empathy, Lavi was a kindred spirit of the Renaissance—a leader, a creative doer, and survivor, whose first ten years of life covered the last decade of a harsh communist regime.

What follows are selected emails from Lavi's extensive email chain during the weeks and months following Chris's death. With discretion, the volume of emails were reduced for purposes of relevancy, privacy, and efficiency. While a few of the emails include dialogue with others, most of those selected are singularly Lavi's voice, as she continued to struggle to make sense of it all.

April 28, 2004. Lavinia's group email one week after Chris died.

> The truth keeps coming to light. I have just read this article I found in the Boston Globe HYPERLINK
> They say that Chris was part of a protective escort to the firefighters from South Carolina. Are you kidding me? He could barely shoot!!! He failed his shooting test in Drum just like many others and he was supposed to protect others? HE was the one to be protected together with other engineers! I am absolutely outraged. I cannot believe this. How can you, smart military people, supposedly with experience, send such inexperienced soldiers, altogether unprotected, in their turn to protect others? Lavinia

April 29, 2004. Lavinia's email to Neal Allen.

> Thank you for your email. I am sorry, I can't write too much. I am not one who lacks words but now I am just speechless. Speechless with rage, fear, grief, and hopelessness. I'd like to talk to you sometime. Lavinia

May 25, 2004. Lavinia's email to Todd Crawford.
Note: Crawford and Alicia Newbegin coordinated the return of Chris's personal belongings to Lavinia.

> Dear Todd,
>
> What a sincere message you wrote to me… I read it over and over again. I still have tears in

my eyes. You really know my Baby. I am glad you wrote because I can feel you are not a stranger to me simply because you knew Chris. I am so sorry I cannot remember you. But I will know you when I see you upon your return to Maine. I forget names but I never forget faces.

You are right about the wedding ring. It will be with me forever. Every time when I am down, I hold the ring and the tag in my left hand and put my right hand over my heart. You know how people talk about "broken hearts" and/or "burning hearts"? I have always thought these phrases were metaphors referring mostly to a state of mind. Well, they are more physical than any bodily pain or ache. When Chaplain Gibson told me on May 20th, "We regretfully inform you…" something just snapped inside my chest, instantly, painfully. It really did. The next second my chest started burning and hurting so much and I remember wanting to jump off that Armory window to put an end to it. It still burns and if I put my hand close to my chest, on its left side, I can feel heat coming out. The only time the burning and the pain went away was on the first day of the wake.

They told me it was not advisable to see Baby. My whole body started burning when they told me. I made up two CD's with our favorite songs and I had the funeral home play them throughout the wake. I don't really remember going inside that wake room as I couldn't feel myself. However, when I wrapped my arms around the flag-draped casket and I laid my chest where I thought Cutie's chest would be, the burning went away. My heart was still broken but it wasn't burning any more. From 3 to 8pm that Thursday and Friday I didn't leave the casket for more than half an hour in total. I felt Baby was holding me both during the wake and the funeral. I had strength to stand up in front of 600 people and talk to Chris and about Chris. That said, I talked for almost half an hour and that I spoke very coherently. I had nothing written down nor did I need anything to express my thoughts. I don't know how long I talked for nor did I see anyone in the audience. I didn't do it for anyone there but for my Sweetie. I was even able to play and sing our song for him. (Right here waiting for you—Richard Marx). I had never played my guitar for him because I only play and sing when I am sad. With him I was always happy and I never felt the need to sing. My heart was broken but I could still sing. People thought I was strong. I wasn't. Chris was holding me.

The burning went away only those 3 days. Now it's back to stay. It's worse at night. I wake up almost every night at 2am when Chris was killed. I have horrifying dreams, most of them involving the feeling of burning or being burned alive.

Thank you, deeply!

August 7, 2004. Lavinia's email to David Wilkinson.

Dear Dave (can I call you Dave?)

Thank you so very much for your message. It means a lot to me that you took the time to write. I know a lot of people want to write to me but they can't find the words. I understand. Chris and I have been together for 3 years and out of those 3 years, he spent 4 months away from me, with the 133rd. That is 1/9th of our time of knowing each other, which is quite significant.

I therefore welcome all accounts of what Chris did or said while he was with you guys. A couple of other Headquarters Support Company folks have written to show their support and they made such a difference. It seems to me that they are the only ones who have a clue of what I am going through. The only people here who keep in touch and always ask how they can help are Linda Newbegin, coordinator of the Family Support Group, Chaplain Gibson and maybe one or two other wives.

For the families left behind in Maine, I represent their worst nightmare, something they don't want to think about if they can help it. I don't blame them. What I am going through IS a nightmare. However, the soldiers over there, who have no choice but to face the facts, have a different approach, plus they knew Chris. Some of them write to me regularly, which I am so grateful for. I know that with time more people will write. May I ask where you got my email address from? You mentioned SGT Moody in your email. If you see him, please send him my warmest regards. He was the person whom Chris was most emotionally attached to within the HSC. Chris kept a journal while he was deployed. SGT Moody's name appears in almost every entry of the journal.

It wasn't just moral support that I received from the soldiers of the 133rd but also reassurance that Chris' personal effects were dealt with care and respect. SSG Fitch, for instance, was one of the people who helped pack Chris' things and who writes often to make sure I am doing ok. 1st LT Crawford took a lot of his time to explain to me what happened to Chris' dog tags, how his personal effects were handled. He was patient, compassionate, and explained things to me until they sank in. CPT Curtis helped a lot in the process as well. SFC Keene took time to write a moving note accompanying my last letter to Chris that I sent on April 20th before I was notified of the ambush. There are other soldiers who wrote and shared their losses of loved ones with me. I am thankful to all who wrote and will write.

Thank you for letting me know about you being with Chris on the way to Baghdad. I know it is painful for you to remember all this. Did Chris move at all, did he open his eyes? Did he say anything? I didn't see him. They said it was not advisable. I didn't see him, I couldn't hold him.

Chris and I emailed daily and talked every morning on the Yahoo Instant Messenger. In his only letter to me, which I received after his death, Chris addressed me as "My one and only true love." He is my everything, the darling baby face in whose eyes the sun seems to have risen forever; a sun that set too soon, leaving darkness over my whole being, a darkness that blinds my eyes.

Of course I would like to meet you when you return. I'd like to meet all of you who knew Chris and loved him. I wrote a poem for all of you. I sent it to some people I knew so you may have read it already.

To the 133rd and all other deployed soldiers with lots of love, from Lavinia.

August 10, 2004

Hi Neal,

Today I am so excited. I have finally written my poem for Chris. He is so special that words just never came to express my love for him in a poem. I'll print it, then have it laminated and I'll put it at his grave. I want to share and celebrate his love for me with those who knew him. I want everybody to know that he was one in a million, my husband and my best friend... Lavi

To My Cutie

We've never said "good-bye," my Baby,
I thought it brought bad luck and sorrow;
We lived for "now" and not for "maybe," Who knew there'll be no tomorrow? "Death doesn't scare me," You said,
"If you are with me nearby"
I tried, my Love, but no steps led
To You and heaven, Cutie Pie...
As I am making hearts of flowers
On your fresh grave, with tremendous hands, I wonder who, like You, for hours
Will kiss my face? Who understands?
Who's gonna lay His head on my chest,
Each morning when bad dreams still linger?
Who's gonna say He's got the best
Under the tip of His small finger?
Who's gonna bake me chocolate cookies
And rub my belly when I stretch?
Who's gonna watch with me fun movies
And ask me if His clothes do match?
Who's gonna tell me about the good days
And kiss my forehead when I'm sad?
Who's gonna love me now and always
Through health, sickness, times good or bad? I'll never say "good-bye," my Baby, However hard I'm hit by sorrow,
Thus "nighty-night," my Love, and maybe I'll live my dream with You tomorrow...

IF YOU LOVE SOMEONE, YOU MUST TELL THEM

Lavinia returns to Sibiu

For two weeks in September of 2004, just five months after Chris died and just when Lavi was beginning to break through to the other side, a family emergency called her back to Romania to help her brother. Their father was in the hospital with a serious self-inflicted injury. True to her strength and compassionate spirit, Lavi put her fragile life on hold in order to be of help for her family.

During her time back in Sibiu, Lavi continued to communicate with me and others. Her emails described the outdated protocols of hospital rules, family visitations, and life in Sibiu, both past and present. Following the revolution of 1989 and its end to the Ceausescu reign, progressive voices began to break through the shield of centuries-old attitudes about relationships and mental illness. Reminders of that past were in stark contrast to the gentle, loving care and support that defined Lavi's relationship with Chris. Her writings reflected the anguished pain in losing her husband and friend, captured in these simple words, "I miss Chris so much… I wish I could just be in his arms and hear him tell me everything will be ok. I cried for two weeks now… I feel so miserable and I miss my baby so much."

September 13, 2004. Lavinia's email from Sibiu, Romania.

> Dear Neal,
>
> It's midnight again here and I am in an internet cafe as usual. I am so sorry, but I do not recall if I told you anything about my father's situation. I am just writing what is going on now. If I haven't written to you before this message, let me know and I'll update you.
>
> I don't know about my father anymore. I told him what's waiting for him if he doesn't recover. It's almost like he understands now but after five minutes you have to say it all over again.

You know what? You'll laugh when you hear this!!! Today I got out of the hospital at 7pm when the doctor came to see the patients. That's how they do it here. Relatives as well as patients are too stupid to know what the doctor's finding are.

Anyway, there's a pretty park right across from the hospital. They have some nice sprinklers there and water changes color especially at night. However, the nicest thing about this park is the ten swings it has. There are so many happy kids swinging on the swings. They are just so worry-less and innocent. I like watching them. I also love the swings. Well, the second kid got off and there was a vacant swing, I took it. As I swayed and listened to Simon and Garfunkel, suddenly there's this angry cop in front of me. Apparently there's a law in our city that prevents adults from using the swings because we are heavier and will ruin them. He wanted to fine me but I had no money on me. I had no documents on me either because I'm always afraid someone will steal them away from me and then I'm stuck here. I had to persuade the policeman that I meant no harm, that I haven't been in the country for a while and that I won't get on the swings anymore. He gave me such a hard time.

I am already looking forward to coming back to the U.S., but then again there's nobody waiting for me there. I am afraid of Halloween, my b-day and Chris' b-day in between these days and after. How weird is that? Best, Lavinia

September 14, 2004.

Dear Neal,

Today the situation got worse. By the time I made it to the hospital, my dad was gone. Nobody let us know that my father was moved to the psychiatry unit, which was really far away. I got really upset but couldn't say anything.

He tried to get out of his room in the neurology section and he fell and cut his left ear. The doctors there had enough of him so they moved him to the psychiatry unit, where he is now. I am not sure that my father will ever be well. I miss Chris so much... I wish I could just be in his arms and hear him tell me everything will be ok. I cried for 2 weeks now... I feel so miserable and I miss my Baby so much I feel like I fell into a dump hole and no matter which direction I turn my head, I still smell the garbage. I am so tired of it. Best always, Lavinia

October 16, 2004. Lavinia's group email. (Lavi returned to Maine in late September.)

Just a quick note today. I think I might have just survived my B-Day... The day is almost over... Thank God! What a horrible day. Lavi

December 13, 2004. Lavinia's email to Owen Swift.

Hello Owen,

You probably don't remember me... I am Chris' wife. As I am now using Chris' laptop, I activated his email by mistake and I guess there was a message Chris never got a chance to send you that was sitting in his outbox. The second I opened his Outlook Email that message was sent to you. I am writing 'cause I don't want you to get freaked when you receive that email. I wish you and all your fellow soldiers to come back home safe. Although Chris is no longer there, I am still connected to all of you.

Best, Lavinia

December 18, 2004. Lavinia's group email.

Dear friends,

    Finally, Chris' headstone is done. I hope he can see it.

    I put lots of love and thought into it, starting with the design and ending with the lyrics that I wrote for Chris on my B-day. The color of the stone is India red (a kind of dark burgundy, like my hair and my car :)) although, in the pics I've taken, you can't really tell because it was at sunset that I took them.

    Let me end with a funny little story. A couple of months ago, somebody asked me why I wanted Chris' stone to be red… I told that person what happened when my father-in-law was about to buy Chris and me the Ford Focus I now have. It was pretty much up to me to choose the color as Chris was really laid back about these kind of things. I asked him while we were chatting online (me—at my desk, he on a computer in Mosul) what color he thought our car should be. On the computer camera, I could see his face light up with a large, warm smile after which he laughed whole heartedly and said "Babe, it can only be red!" I laughed and felt like pinching his cheeks. He knew his wife all too well.

If I had asked Chris even before I put in the order what color the stone should be ('cause it's going to be my stone when I join him), he would put on the same candid smile and say, "Babe it can only be red..." Best to all, Lavi

December 21, 2004. *Portland Press Herald*: MOSUL SUICIDE ATTACK KILLS 22 INCLUDING 2 FROM MAINE'S 133rd.[1]

Almost eight months to the day of the death of Chris Gelineau, the 133rd was faced with more tragedy and death. It was four days before Christmas, December 21, 2004, when Bill Nemitz of the *Portland Press Herald*, who was back on assignment covering the 133rd, opened his report back to Maine with the tragic news: "A powerful explosion ripped through a crowded dining facility at Forward Operating Base Marez during the noon lunch hour Tuesday killing 22 people and wounding 66."

Among the eighteen Americans killed, two were with Maine's 133rd Engineering Battalion: Sergeant Lynn R. Poulin Sr., forty-seven, of Freedom, Maine, a welder at Bath Iron Works in his civilian life; and Specialist Thomas John Dostie, twenty, who had grown up in Somerville. Five civilian American contractors were killed, together with three Iraqi security force members and the suicide bomber. The wounded included twelve members of the 133rd, two with serious injuries, but all survived.

In addition to the 133rd, the dining facility at FOB Marez serviced a large contingent of soldiers from the First Brigade, Twenty-Fifth Infantry Division, based at Fort Lewis, Washington. Brigadier General Carter Ham,[2] commander of Operation Iraqi Freedom's Northern Task Force Olympia, called it the "worst day in my life." Of his initial reaction, he said, "I got there about thirty minutes after the explosion and what I saw was American soldiers doing what they do best, taking care of each other." Ham would later cite the mess hall event as the source of his own battle with post-traumatic stress disorder (PTSD). In seeking treatment for his condition, he publicly encouraged soldiers to do the same.

Years later in a conversation with me, Sergeant First Class Alicia Newbegin recalled in chilling detail her experience that day. Newbegin, who served as the operations sergeant for the Headquarters Staff Company (HSC), the same company that Chris Gelineau served in, explained that she rarely ever went to the DFAC (dining facility) for lunch. Her preference was to remain in the office to allow her younger staff to break together as a unit for the noontime meal. On December 21, Newbegin's assistant staff sergeant, Roger Jones, encouraged her to go to lunch with all her staff, including First Lieutenant Todd Crawford. In spite of Newbegin's anxiety, she agreed to join the group for lunch. On arriving at the DFAC, the group chose a table toward the back of the facility.

Newbegin, who unabashedly watched over the younger soldiers, felt a sixth sense of unease as they worked their way through lunch. As a strong and devout Christian, she suddenly felt God was trying to send her a message. As her anxiety grew, her sense of foreboding grew in lockstep, and she said in no uncertain terms, "We have to get out." Instead of exiting via the main entrance, which was further away from where they were seated, Newbegin directed the group to the closer rear exit. Shortly after they emerged from the DFAC, a suicide bomber who had been sitting close to them activated his vest bomb.[3]

Newbegin's account of that day is confirmed by Todd Crawford, who served as the Headquarters Support Company executive officer (XO). The following is Crawford's description of that day.[4]

> We waited a long time to eat, and I recognized the company of Iraq trainee soldiers in line a short way behind us. We sat at a table closest to the serving area midway between both ends (the DFAC was a long oval tent). There were other soldiers from our company seated around us, including Tommy Dostie. I absolutely, 100% recall Alicia not being comfortable. As soon as we finished eating, she insisted that we leave.

Not one to argue with gut feelings, I agreed. We walked outside, through barriers and across the street. When we got just past the intersection, we heard the boom. We were all stunned. I shoved Alicia and the other soldiers to the ground at the side of the road. I could see the big black cloud of smoke rising above the DFAC.

I knew this was no ordinary random attack. As we just started to head to our company area, we saw and heard soldiers running towards DFAC yelling, "For any Combat Lifesavers to DFAC." Alicia instinctively wanted to head back to the DFAC. My head said the same, but I remembered the mass casualty plan. Alicia was key in that plan, because she had to sound the alarm and initiate the plan into action. I yelled to her to get to Operations and execute the mass-cal plan. She ran to Operations. I followed, but started making the calls on my hand-held radio.

The plan worked very well. Thank goodness we had this plan and exercised it. (Note: Together with the Battalion Surgeon, the mass casualty plan was developed by Crawford and rehearsed a few times). We pulled about a dozen wounded, bleeding soldiers from various types of vehicles skidding into our medical station casualty area. One included SGT Chris Rushlau from our company. He had a chest wound. I will never forget seeing Chris and pulling him from the vehicle. It really hit home then.

After a while, I called the company to execute a headcount for accountability of all our soldiers. We (HSC—our company) were missing one: Tommy Dostie. I calmed everyone and said to be patient. Hopefully, he will appear. I had the company scouring for Tommy, and I kept reassuring everyone that we will find him. Not too long later, I was informed that Tommy was at the medical hospital (just to the east of the Mosul airfield). He did not survive. I had to inform the platoon and section sergeants.

As a follow-up to Crawford's description of the event, sixteen years later, the 133rd Battalion commander, John Jansen, would tell me that the suicide bomber had been employed on the base for many months and over that time, had gained the confidence of the soldiers as a local who could be trusted. For perspective, FOB Marez was a very large facility with thousands of people entering and exiting throughout the day. Whether the bomber entered the base that day, hugged by a vest of explosives, or it was assembled by others who smuggled it on to the base was never determined to my knowledge.

Once again, the men and women of the 133rd assembled to pray and remember and to honor and respect two of their own. And once again, the sad ritual—empty boots, dog tags, helmet, and weapon rested at the altar to the haunting roll call for Sergeant Poulin and Specialist Dostie. Within two months of their arrival, they had come together in grief for Chris Gelineau, and now with two months remaining in their deployment, they were there to do the same for Lynn Poulin and Tom Dostie. Chris and Tom totaled just forty-three years of life between them—a number not even exceeding the still-young Lynn Poulin. All three had so much more to give and live for. Whoever first said, "Only the good die young," must have seen it firsthand in war.

Lavinia was devastated when informed of the December 21 attack. Not only did it bring back in full focus the horror and grief of losing her Chris, but she could feel the pain that was piercing the hearts of the loved ones of Lynn Poulin and Tom Dostie.

December 22, 2004. Lavinia's email to soldiers of the 133rd.

> Only eight months later and tragedy hits again. My mind is empty. I did a lot of crying today. When I read about the attack in Mosul today, I felt like somebody was telling me again

that Chris had been killed. All of a sudden my arms went numb, I felt very cold, started shaking and having a hard time breathing. Then I cried, and cried and then I ran to the armory in Portland. I didn't know where else to go, who to tell how I felt 'cause nobody really wants to hear.

As I am typing this email, I am thinking with horror that about 480 families in Maine are waiting to see if the Chaplain is gonna knock at the door tonight... God, that hurts... I remember that so well. *This is the lottery nobody wants to win.* I don't think I'll be able to sleep tonight so I'll just get drunk. I can't handle this. I went to the grocery store today to get some food and some people were laughing... How could they laugh? Haven't they seen the news? I got so mad I just wanted to beat everybody up.

Please let me know if you are OK. I am thinking of, and praying for all of you. I asked Chris to watch over the other soldiers and help make their transition to the other world smoother. I know he'll be there for them. Peace, Lavinia

December 22, 2004. Lavinia's email to Kevin Pillsbury.

Hi Kevin,

I noticed you posted this message on the fallen heroes website.

"You will be missed for all that you were. You were my friend every weekend. I pray for your family every day. Until we meet again."

How well did you know Chris? Are you in Iraq? Please share with me any memories you have of Chris if you can. It's very important to me. Thank you for the kind words. I don't know if you knew that but there's another website with photos that's dedicated to Chris, aside from the military one.

Peace, Lavinia

Hello Lavinia,

Well let me first start by apologizing for not writing or calling you. I don't have an excuse, so I won't try. I joined the Army about the same times Chris, in 1998. As you know he had a job in the military that made him a well-known soldier. We would talk about school, the military, as well as doing administrative things like setting up MY PAY accounts. We also talked about you. He was the youngest person that I knew who was married. I remember a time that I asked him why he got married so very young. He told me that he knew he was in love, and that it was an easy decision.

I have all good memories of Chris. I think the most prevalent ones come from his smile. When I first heard about his death, it was the only way I could picture him. Sitting in his chair behind his desk with a grin from ear to ear. I remember how he was the *Guidon Bearer* for the Company. Every promotion I got, he was standing right there next to me, giving my first congratulations. He was a great person. Although I did not know him socially, only through the Guard, I feel blessed to have even met him.

I hope this letter reaches you in good health. Ben Leonard is one of my closest Army friends, some time we should all get together. I know he was running the FAC for a time, and he tells me he stays in contact with you. Sorry for not contacting you. Kevin

IF YOU LOVE SOMEONE, YOU MUST TELL THEM

Kevin

    Please tell everybody that I am glad to receive messages, to hear stories about Chris or just you guys are doing… I also wrote a poem dedicated to all of you and I sent it to a couple of the people whose names I knew from Chris' journals… It describes how hard it was to say good-bye last January 5 in Gardiner… I still remember the day like it was today… Could you please print this poem and put it on a wall so people can see it and know it's dedicated to them? It's my way of saying Thank You… Lavinia

    I was so glad to hear from you! What you told me about Chris is so important to me. Thank you for sharing. I think Ben told me about you. I just didn't make the connection.

    I would like to meet you sometime after the holidays. Maybe you and Ben can come over sometime or we can go out.

    Please keep in touch.

    My best, Lavi

    You're in the Army Now

    They wear kevlar vests and carry M16's

    It's not a dream they're dreaming and they must take a stand;

    Some kiss their wives good-bye; some barely seventeen,

    Haven't yet walked the aisle or held a girlfriend's hand…

    And they must board a bus… The bugle plays a song

    "You're in the Army Now"… The driver beeps the horn

    "I love you, Babe, for ever… I won't be gone for long!"

Their tears freeze, their babies cry when from their arms they're torn… Eyes closed, fists clenched, they take their seats real slow…

"May God be with you and please write a letter when you can,"

A young wife sobs… "I'll be back home before you know,"

Her green-eyed Cutie smiles, "And then, we'll live again…"

Much love and warmest thoughts,
Lavinia

December 24, 2004. Lavinia's email to Christina Lewis.

Chrissy.

I am over at my parents in law in VT and I received your email, message, and photo of Chris with an open heart and tears in my eyes. I was wondering if I could get the actual picture that you scanned and maybe mail it to me… I'd like to have it close to me and maybe even frame it. The scanned copy isn't very clear and I can't really make out some of the writing. It means so much to me that you guys are thinking of me… This is the most beautiful present anyone would have been able to give me. Best always, Lavi

December 28, 2004. Lavinia's email to Mike Bennett.

Hi Mike,

Thank you for the wishes. Are you heading to Iraq again to bring back soldiers?

Yesterday I went to Borders and bought 2 copies of "Embraced by the Light" and 2 copies of "five People You Meet in Heaven," a copy for each family of the 2 soldiers. Those 2 books have helped me some during the grieving process. I'll probably donate some money to help them like others helped me when Chris passed; just have to check my bank account to see what my balance is. I just paid $3,000 for the remaining balance for Chris' stone and the bills.

I am also writing a poem for these families. Everybody close to me said that going to these 2 funerals will hurt me a lot and suggested I should reconsider going. I know it's gonna hurt me a lot but I have to go. I mean I don't have to, but somehow inside me I know I need to go and be of support if I can. Both of these families live 2 hours north away from me so I hope the weather will be good this week. Ah, on Thursday, in the afternoon I am also going to a wake of one of the soldiers.

Best always, Lavi

December 29, 2004. Lavinia's email to Todd Crawford.

Hi Todd,

The next 2 days will be hard. I'll go to the funeral and the wake tomorrow and to another funeral on Friday. I don't have to go but I want to. I feel deep inside I have to… I need to show my support and be there. I'll take the day off. I'm glad you like my poetry. The last thing I wrote was a poem dedicated to a 21 year old student who died 2 weeks ago. I had Chris in mind too when I wrote it.

Here it is:

I tried to follow close and catch you Before you fell into the light;

But who am I to be so selfish

And bring you back into the night?

They say that "there" you feel no sorrow, No weight, no pain—just pure bliss; I'm selfish, still, and hope tomorrow

You'll wake me up with your warm kiss…

January 1, 2005. Lavinia's dedication to Tommy Dostie and Lynn Poulin.

A new year started. I kept hearing people wishing each other a "Happy New Year" and I envied them because for me and many others in my shoes, it's just gonna be a new year. Happiness? It's like an obsolete word I hate hearing. Anyway, I thought a lot about the families who have lost their soldiers on Dec 21st.

On Thursday I went to the service for SGT Poulin and the same day I went to the wake of SPC Dostie. I never met them or their families but that's not important. I kept wondering if these families will ever be able to have a "Happy New Year" given that they buried their loved ones on New Year's Eve. I mean it's hard enough to lose your soldier as it is, let alone having to go through the initial shock and crisis at a time when everybody is looking forward to opening presents and going to parties.

Wednesday night I kept thinking about what I was gonna say to the families when I saw them. I felt I had lots to say but I wasn't able to write anything that made sense. What was I gonna say? "Be strong," "Keep your chin up," "Hang in there?" I still don't know what people mean, if anything, when they say those expressions to me.

Chris' loss was brought very close to me once more. I lay on my couch, thinking of Chris, Lynn, and Tommy.

I wrote a poem in their honor.

A breath, a smile, hurried glances,
Another breath and You were gone
Oh, God! Not you!" What were the chances
That You would be the chosen one?
"We regretfully inform you…" Darkness fell… In just one second, just one breath,
My peaceful life shook hands with Hell,
My dreams burned down in sudden death…
And as I closed my teary eyes,
An unseen hand brushed off my fear…
I felt Your light and realized
You are so close to me, so near!

January 21, 2005. Lavinia's email to Hal Fitch.

Hi Hal,

It's been awhile since I last emailed you. Lately I've been very busy, which I guess is a good thing. I am under contract for a house in Westbrook. I'll attach some photos of it… I didn't take my photos of the inside 'cause it's not finished. It has a 3/4 bathroom, dining room, kitchen, living room and a bedroom on the first floor, and 3 bedrooms and a bathroom on the second floor. It looks pretty neat, just the way I would want it. My mom can have the first floor and I can have the second floor. Yesterday I had to go pick the linoleum and the carpets. That was tough and not exciting as I was supposed to do that with Chris not by myself. Lavi

Hal responded.

Dear Lavinia!

    It is so good to hear from you my friend. I feel so bad for not emailing back sooner, there is not a day that goes by that I don't think about you and Chris. I wanted you to know that first of all I feel a big congratulations is in hand for you about buying your new home. I know it must be difficult because you and Chris were to do that but I feel he is and helped you through this process and I imagine he is smiling down own on you and would have been very proud of what you have done. The pictures of the house look great, even though it isn't finished yet it will all come together soon and will look awesome! I'm very happy for you for pursuing your Master's degree, that is a huge milestone in anyone's book and I know you'll do great.
    On questions about me, I have been okay but feel so drained lately with all the work going on and thinking of coming home at the same time. At this point it seems so overwhelming that I can't sleep. I sometimes have good dreams and bad dreams at night. It keeps me awake and I can't sleep and its hard to catch up on your sleep especially if you are tagged for duty the next day.
    I did have a dream about you and Chris about a week ago. I was at a museum just looking at the painting on the wall, admiring the detail and definition of the work that goes into creating

such a wonderful piece. I felt a tap on my shoulder and when I turned around you and Chris were standing there asking me if I knew who painted the painting. I said I don't know who the artist was but what really stunned me was that it was a painting of a sailboat with a picture of the shoreline in the background with a lighthouse. You and Chris noted that you have been there before and that was one of your favorite places to visit.

Chris introduced himself as Chris and he said this is my wife Lavi. I shook Chris' hand and said my name is Hal and after a brief introduction you both looked into each others eyes and smiled at another and said it was nice to meet you. You both turned and started to walk away and you stopped and said to me, "Please be safe and the rest will take care of itself." I really didn't know what you meant by that comment but I said, thank you and you both walked away. That was where it ended. When I had this dream it seemed so real especially when I shook Chris' hand. It just felt that I was actually shaking it. I can't explain why I dreamt that but all I know is that it seemed so real.

For the time frame coming back it looks like sometime between the end of February and the beginning of March, that is all I know. When you mentioned Chris being gone for nine months I remembered it yesterday. I have a copy of his memorial taped to the inside of my wall locker and have had it there since I went to his memorial service at Merez. I look at every day when I open my wall locker. It helps me to have it there and how much of a good friend he was and for me to make sure he is not forgotten. I will keep in touch more often when this month is over. We are so busy until then but I will try to email as often as I can. Again, congratulations on your new home and I am very excited for you!! Take care my friend and will always be in touch. Hal.

January 22, 2005. San Pao's email to Lavinia.

Hi there. I'm doing ok. Making it as I might say. It's almost over, this deployment is all too long. Lol. I'm packing and sending packages home this week, so what does all that tell you? I don't know the date of when I'll arrive back home, but March is definitely the month I'll come home safe and sound. At least safe anyway. Send me a pic of you or however many you want to send back if any at all. Sincerely, San. God speed!

Lavi responded

I know you guys will be coming back around the time I will be moving into the new place. I am dreading that time. I am becoming more and more emotional. I miss my husband and I want him here with me. Choosing a home, picking the rugs and the furniture was something we were supposed to do together. I just want to move in and that's it… I am not excited about it. I am just taking a step, supposedly a forward one.

Also, I need to get back to school. With what I'm earning at present, I won't be able to offer a decent life to my child. I will try to get my MA in ESL or French and start teaching.

Today I started packing some tapes and some of Chris' CD's. I cried the whole day. I'm gonna have a beautiful house to admire by myself. What good is that to me? Someone at work told me she envies me for getting this home. I told her not to, 'cause she doesn't know what price was paid for it…

I miss my husband, I miss my best friend, I miss feeling alive. On Valentine's Day it will have been one year since I last saw Chris… No wonder lately the only things I remember about him physically, are static image, snapshots of his smile… I can't remember him in motion sometimes…

Best, Lavi. PS. And as proof that sometimes I can smile, I'll attach a very recent photo of me and my kitty, Sasha, that Chris and I brought home from the shelter 2 days before Chris left for Fort Drum

January 23, 2005. Lavinia's email to Mathew Delk.

Dear CPT Delk,

One of Chris' relatives had a very interesting experience regarding Chris. I just haven't been in the right state of mind to talk about that but I may be now. Her name is Pam and she is the wife of one of Chris' stepdad's brothers. In my opinion, she has psychic abilities although she says she's no a psychic. It actually freaks her out. Every once in a while, a spirit will visit her. She's an educated woman and has a lot of common sense. Most often the spirits visiting her are somehow related to her. For the most part it's been her brother, a 20-year old Navy soldier who died about 8 years ago. He came one day, while she was ironing some clothes and was by herself.

She couldn't see him but she could feel him. The way the spirits "talk" to her and the way she communicates with them is through her mind. That day her brother asked her to tell their father 3 things. She hesitated saying anything to her dad as she thought it was just her imagination.

Months later she asked her dad if those 3 things made any sense to him. It turns out that the father had asked her brother, Jason, those 3 questions only 3 months before he died and that those 3 things were the answers. This is not the only instant when she had this kind of experience. The dead father on one of her best friends contacted her too.

When I found out about her abilities I asked if she could talk to Chris. Initially she said that she didn't dare ask spirits to come to her. They normally come by themselves. She was afraid to initiate the whole thing. However, one day as she was making some teeth (she's a dentist's technician) she could feel a spirit's presence around. This was the Tuesday before Thanksgiving. Instantly she thought of Chris and without really thinking about it, she called onto him. She said that the second she called on Chris, he was there. She said that that was the very first time when she could distinguish a face and she could see Chris' face so clearly. She grabbed a pen and some paper to write things down. She said that Chris was there for about 3 hours and he was making great effort to communicate to her all he had to say. Pam said that it was extremely difficult for her to understand and therefore, Chris had to repeat the same thing over and over again.

Here is what Chris told her as close as possible to his words.

1) "Tell Lavi and my mom that I didn't feel anything."
2) "It's ok about the cat; we're together." Pam didn't know this but right after Chris died, Chris' cat fell really ill and my mom had to put her to sleep.
3) He asked Pam to tell me that he misses my smile and that I should smile more and not cry so much. He said, "You are so beautiful."
4) He said something about Philip, which Pam could not understand. Again, Pam didn't know this name; even I didn't. Philip was my mom-in-law's brother who died in an accident when he was very young,
5) He also said that if I decide to have his baby, he'd rather I didn't name him or her after Chris, which is exactly what I would have done. Chris or Christina as a middle name would be ok. So Pam asked him if he had any suggestions in mind. He said "Carmen Victoria" if it's a girl and "Lucas Christopher" if it's a boy. Then Chris said something about 2 in regards to children which prompted Pam to believe he was talking twins. Nobody but Chris and I had ever had this conversation, Whenever Chris and I would talk about kids, I would always say that I only want 1 baby, that's all. Chris would get very passionate and say that we really should have 2 kids;

he was the only child and grew up very lonely. Plus, if something should happen to us, the brother would have each other.
6) The other thing Chris asked Pam to tell me was that this was the way it was meant to be for him to die at 23. That I should not be afraid because things will be fine. He said that a while will go by and I will remarry and be happy again.
7) The last thing he told her was that now his role is to help other soldiers who die in the war make the transition.

I think this is all he said. Pam told me that she was jotting things down while listening to Chris., she wrote, "Chris doesn't want Lavi to… or Lavi shouldn't…" Every time she would try to write down one of those phrase starters, Chris would correct her and tell her, "Don't tell Lavi she should or shouldn't." This is very much like Chris because he never imposed anything on me and never ever asked me to do things. He always suggested and tried to guide me if he could but never told me I should or shouldn't do something.

While Pam was telling me and Vicky, my mom-in-law, about all these things, I asked her if she could call on to Chris. She said Chris was there. Both she and Vicky could feel Chris' presence; I couldn't and I was so upset. Chris' mom can feel his presence very often. I never can. Pam said that I am too distressed and Chris can't get through to me. After all, the majority of what Chris said was a message to me…

After I saw Pam, I got such a sense of peace knowing that Chris hasn't just disappeared in a black hole. It gives me the hope I'll see him again. Some of the anger vanished but the hurt of missing Chris is there with the same intensity.

This is the amazing stuff that I was telling you on the phone. It was such a pleasure talking to you. It helps me a lot, as I said, to talk to the people who were there for Chris.

February 11, 2005. Lavinia's group email.

I wanted to let you all know that as of Feb. 8th, I became an American citizen… I think they must have made an exception for me 'cause they swore me in the same day instead of having me wait another 3 months they swear everyone in as a group. I was grateful that was the last time I had to walk in the INS office… I answered all the history questions correctly, except for one—I couldn't remember the title of the American national anthem although I knew the lyrics and I knew who wrote it… But the INS guy was very nice to me. He told me it starts with "Star" and it ends with "Banner." Peace and love to all, Lavi

February 12, 2005.

Congratulations Lavinia! Happy to see they were accommodating for you. I see in your words that you are struggling—I wish there were something I could do to help ease your pain—know that I pray for you often, and if you just need to vent—let things go—I'm an email away.

The 94th Engineers have started to arrive—it feels great to almost be out of here—can't wait to see my girls—it's been too long. I will be leaving shortly to go to Kuwait—I am on the advance party to Fort Drum, so it won't be long—can't give you any date—OPSEC—but it is getting so close—its very exciting.

Alicia Wilkinson

February 13, 2005. Lavinia's group email.

I woke up this morning wondering, "Can anyone really plan his/her future? Can anyone even try to plan a day in his/her life a year from now?" I thought I could a year ago… Yesterday was a weird day. Actually, the weirdness started on Friday when my boss sent me to Hannaford to get some food for a meeting. I had avoided the stores for about 2 weeks now; I listened to CD's rather than the radio and tried not to watch TV… I was safe for awhile until I had to walk into Hannaford on Friday. I had prepared myself but the view still caught me off-guard. People seemed to have gone crazy… Everybody was getting ready to party. I could count at least 15 bouquets of red roses being checked out at counters while I was waiting in line to pay for my purchase. I tried not to think too much of it but it occurred to me that everybody around me was pretty normal, except for myself.

My mom went to VT to take care of my dad-in-law's parents for a while so I'm now by myself. My mom has been living with me since the funeral. Yesterday was the first day when I washed the dishes and cleaned around my place since April 17, 2004. I started doing the dishes and the second I poured some dish detergent on to the sponge, I felt like a huge void in the upper part of my stomach. That smell, I knew that smell… Chris used to come by, wrap his arms around me, kiss me a couple of times and thank me for doing the dishes. God, I remember that distinctive warmth in my chest that the sound of his voice, the incredible light in his eyes and his smile would make me feel.

I remember how it used to feel to look forward to tomorrow, to look forward to finishing a meal to see if Baby liked it. I was never a good cook, but I loved cooking because Chris loved sharing it with him. Sometimes he would take pictures of the table with the plates steaming on it. He always thought I was doing such a great job and never complained. Sometimes I would complain to him, "Babe, I've been doing the dishes all this last month. When are you gonna do them?" He would look at me with a little devilish smile on his face and say, "Babe, you are doing such a great job. You are doing a much better job that I would so I'll let you do them." Then we would both start laughing and I would run after him to kick his ass. Truth is, he helped me with everything and was very considerate and appreciative of everything I did in the house.

He took nothing for granted. He even made pancakes twice and he made chocolate chip cookies three times. That was really nice of him, especially when I lost my job in 2002 and I thought it was gonna be the end of the world. His chocolate chip cookies helped...

After I finished the dishes and the cleaning, I decided to go to the cemetery to talk to Chris... Forgetful as I am sometimes, I didn't realize it had snowed so much the last couple of days, I didn't bring my boots and my gloves with me. When I got to Chris' grave (he's right near the alley), there was so much snow that one could barely see the headstone. I got so mad and, just as I usually do, I needed to blame someone. The plow guy... He just plowed all that freakin' snow on my Baby's grave... I grabbed my shovel from the trunk and started shoveling. The snow came up to my thighs. Stupid me, snow got in my shoes... I got out of the snow trying to come up with a plan.

As I was standing there, leaning against the shovel and watching the mountain of snow on Chris' grave, my whole body felt torn apart. I thought to myself that just a year before, I was so excited, getting ready to go to Fort Drum to see him. I was concerned with when I was gonna get my hair cut, then when I was gonna get it dyed red, how I was gonna get to Fort Drum (I didn't know how to drive back then), how I was gonna keep the mashed potatoes, meat loaf and cookies from going bad on my way to Fort Drum...

All of a sudden, a year later I was concerned with how to get that huge amount of snow off his grave. Tears started coming out and I became so angry... I held tight onto the shovel and started removing the snow, one shovel worth of snow at a time, being careful at the same time that I not pile all that snow on someone else's grave. I was not gonna let that snow weigh heavy over Chris. 35 minutes later, the job was done. I was really hot, although I couldn't really feel my hands. I felt some relief, but that didn't last long. The headstone was full of ice, especially the base.

The shovel was useless. I knelt with one knee only and looked at the photos of Chris and me that I had placed in the display case. Two beautiful young people who were gonna show the world what true love is. Two people who were gonna grow old together and still walk hand and hand at the age of 80. I remember that day of February 20th, 2004 when the green SUV that brought me to Watertown, NY, stopped in front of Microtel motel. My heart started racing and my hands and my nails began removing the ice off the headstone. I saw Chris waiting for me at the front desk and waiving at me. I almost forgot the food and the cookies in some lady's trunk (she was there to see her hubby too and she gave me a ride; forgot her name). Some more ice came off the stone... Chris welcomed me at the Microtel front desk and I remember looking at him and wondering if I was really there with him. We went to the room we had rented and just hugged for 20 minutes. I was breathless, just feeling Chris' heart pounding, almost coming out of his chest while he was holding me.

Yeah, my Baby was alive, and his heart was racing... I looked at the stone and it was finally clean. I rubbed my hand over it to make sure I had removed all of the little particles of snow left there. There, it was clean and it looked pret—y—a big red heart made of granite that was shining in a cemetery covered with snow. I went back to my car and tried to warm up my hands. They hurt and I had a couple of minor cuts, but it was all worth it. While I was driving back home, I looked at people in other cars when I was waiting for the light to turn green. They probably looked at me, seeing a 25-year-old woman who was sad. To them, I was just another driver going about my business...

Every once in a while, I get the question, "are you married?" Without even thinking, I show my left hand with my wedding and engagement rings on and I say, "Yes." I always get mad when I have to fill forms at the doctor's or for tax purposes and I am being asked for my marital status. I hate the "widowed" category, but if they don't make it available, I'll check "married." When my insurance company raised my car premium by 120% after Chris' death, they tried to say it was because I wasn't married anymore. I argued with the agent on the phone and, in the end, told her to shove her insurance up her ass 'cause I was gonna get it elsewhere. And I did!

You know, in March last year, Chris wrote me a letter that only reached me a week after his death. It was the only paper and pen letter he sent me while he was away. We would talk daily on the Yahoo IM, he would email his daily journal, and he would call me every Sunday. I wanted something tangible from him, so I asked him to write me a real letter. He made a couple of CD's for me, showing me his room and recording himself playing ping-pong and bowling; in the same package, he included a letter. On the envelope, he wrote, "To my one and only true love, Lavi." That's why I am still married to him. He is the only ONE for me as I am the only ONE for him...

Peace, Lavi

February 22, 2005. Lavinia's group email.

Surprise! I'm still alive...
Hi there,

Ok, I'm gonna make a long story short... On my way home from VT yesterday, I-89 was a traffic nightmare. I left my mom-in-law's home at 5:30 am, thinking that I'm not gonna have to deal with lots of drivers so early in the morning,

Traffic was incredibly slow and cars were traveling on the median of the road. There was only one instead of two lanes; as the sides were slippery, people were just driving in the middle. I saw about 4 or 5 cars off the road and kept thinking that if something happened to me, I didn't even have a Will.

I was listening to 92.9 and they were talking about a VT National Guard unit that had just arrived at the Burlington airport from a 13-month deployment in Iraq. Ah, did I mention that all the bridges over the Interstate had big signs welcoming the unit back home? I was angry, not because these soldiers were coming back (God bless them, they were there too long!!!) but because I couldn't put a sign there myself to welcome my Baby home... I felt a knife in my stomach and I tried to turn off the radio station and instead turn on my CD player.

The big truck in front of me seemed to be throwing a huge amount of snow in my direction. The road was slippery and it was snowing a kind of snow I had never seen before; actually it was a thick, heavy rain, that froze the second it touched the ground and the windshields... I was reaching the radio button and at the same time trying to pay attention to the road, when I suddenly couldn't see anything in front of me. May have been the snow being blown off the tires of the truck in from of me or the wind or both, or maybe the tears made my vision blurry too. Despite my knowing that this was the worst thing I could do, I hit the brakes as hard as I could. The back of my car started skidding and the time I took the foot off the brake, my car started spinning.

That split of a second, I thought I was going to die and I felt no fear… My small Ford Focus hit a snow bank on the right side of the road with the driver's side and then it started rolling. I heard the windshield crack and then the car stopped. I was upside down and my seat belt was holding me in place.

I think I might have been in shock because common sense tells you that if you are hanging upside down and you unfasten your seat belt, inertia is going to kick in and you're gonna fall on your head. Well, my smart ass didn't seem to realize that so I did kinda land on my head. Funny, eh? I started swearing (you would think a lady doesn't do that) just lying there but then I thought maybe I should try to get myself out of there just in case my car would explode. There, finally I was thinking somewhat straight for a change… I got out of my car through the passenger door and just wanted to go away. A man who pulled over to help me took me in his car and called 911. So there! Needless to say my car was totaled… The man who towed my car said I was the 7th person he had towed in 2 hours and that his cell had been ringing off the hook. He also said I was the luckiest of the people who were in a similar crash. I told him I thought I was lucky too and I knew why Chris was there, making sure nothing would happen to me. The paramedics wondered too at the way my car hit the snow and the way I wasn't injured at all.

A couple of miles down the road, where there were ditches and trees the people who went off the road there, were taken to the ER. Hours later, when my dad-in-law came to pick me up, as we were driving from Lebanon, NH (where my car went off the road) and Manchester, NH, we saw at least 10 accidents. I-295 was closed because 12 cars were involved in a single accident and traffic couldn't resume for hours.

So for now, I'm just driving an ugly purple Chevy Impala that I rented… Horrible car but it serves its purpose.

Peace, Lavi

Lavi's account of her car crash in the snow reflected another dimension to her personality and character. She enjoyed telling a funny story or two and all the better if it was of the self-deprecating kind. In closing one of her difficult, emotional experiences, Lavi transitioned with the following:

Ok, to end on a funnier note, here's what happened when I tried to drive a different car than mine. Today I had to take some DVD's back to the rental store and when I came out of there, I got into the car and noticed that my key wouldn't go in the contact. I tried patiently and it still wouldn't do it. "What the heck," I thought, "it just worked 5 minutes ago." Suddenly, I feel the smell of french fries… I look on the passenger's seat and there was a big Burger King bag with steaming food in it. SHit, I was in someone else's car. I got out right away and walked to my car, also red, also a Ford, but it was a different Ford model. At this point I started laughing and laughing until my jaw hurt. But I guess the adventure is over 'cause the sales guy is bringing my car back in about 20 minutes.

IF YOU LOVE SOMEONE, YOU MUST TELL THEM

March 6, 2005. Lavinia's email to Leslie Scribner.

Hi Leslie,

Thanks for your kind words. Today at 3 pm, as buses full of 133rd soldiers are pulling in to their armories, I will be closing on a house in Westbrook. What a screwy deal! These ladies are getting their husbands back; I am getting a house.
Love to you, Travis, and the little one, Lavi

Dear Lavi,

A house? That is wonderful. Well as always there are advantages and disadvantages but either way, something to call your own. We would love to come see you sometime. We were going to plan a trip this summer for a weekend or something…we wanted to touch base with you while you were in the area. We want to come see Chris' grave and hopefully touch base with you. We will let you know around that time farm to see if you may have a day free. I wish you the best of luck with your house. A big responsibility but well worth the effort. Please let us know if we can do anything to help!
With love, Leslie

The return to Fort Drum in early March 2005 was a bittersweet moment for the men and women of the 133rd. Deaths, injuries, and the constant stress of living and working in a distant war zone within a distinctly different region of the world carried memories and emotional scars that would shadow the members of the battalion for the rest of their lives. While they were happy to be returning, the joy and excitement of reuniting with family and friends was tempered with the news that Sgt. Michael Jones had fallen seriously ill, with a rapidly declining medical condition that was not attributed to his year in Iraq. As his conditioned worsened, Jones was transferred to a hospital in Syracuse, New York. Surrounded by his wife Lori Jones and family who had come to welcome him home, Jones died just days away from his forty-fourth birthday. Battalion Commander John Jansen, who remained by Lori's side, remembers Michael Jones as a "tremendous soldier who was respected and loved by all." Promoted to first sergeant (SFC) posthumously, Jones received many awards over his military career including a Bronze Star.

March 8, 2005. Lavinia's email to MD Mitchell.

Dear Mitch,

> I am so busy and stressed and so tired. I am moving out on Saturday and I still have everything packed… Tomorrow I will attend SGT Jones funeral in Augusta. Will you be there? I will be coming with SGT McKinney 'cause I still don't have a car.
> Thank you for being my friend throughout this long, painful year! You have helped me more than you can ever imagine! How can I help you? When are you going back to Fort Drum? Will you have surgery then?
> Peace and love,
> Lavi

> Dear Lavinia, I heard through the email grapevine that you are all set with a ride. Heather was going to offer but others had already stepped up to help. That works too. Heather is in Walpole, that would have been a challenge.
> I am back at Ft. Drum, came back today… long drive…yuck…luckily there was not as much snow as was forecast. I will not be able to attend

the funeral… I heard it is going to be a challenge to get SFC Jones to his funeral as well because of the weather, apparently they were going to fly him back but the weather cancelled the flight… so apparently the General sent a couple guys and a vehicle to pick him up in Syracuse and drive through the night to bring him home… I hear they will get a police escort most of the way… he is a good man, Chris will have good company with him.

I am glad I could help you. You asked what you could do for me…gee…not sure…for now, just good thoughts would help. My wife, Heather, is feeling a bit lonely too…if you would like to call and invite her to something, that would be lovely too, but only if you really want to. She wanted to go to a movie tonight, but the weather was too icky out.

Not really sure about what will happen medically, I have an appointment tomorrow, but that is only to see about where they will send me next. I am hoping surgery will not happen soon, but who knows? I think they will send me to Walter Reed. I will keep you posted. When I get back, I would like to find time to get together if that would be good for you.

Hugs, Love, Mitch

Dear Lindsey,

I am sorry I keep failing to answer your emails promptly. I am in such a hurry to pack all my stuff by Saturday and I have so much going on at work and at home, that my mind is just not there for anything else. I know you probably told me when that conference took place. I just can't find that email right now.

Also, I am not sure if you knew that, but right after April 20th I started speaking out against the war and gave numerous interviews with the newspapers and TV stations. One article was published by the Associated Press all over the US. If there are other war widows around, 99% of them will be offended by my views... I wonder if me speaking there would be a good idea... Let me know what you think...

Peace, Lavi

Dear Lavinia,

The conference is on September 11th in Washington, DC and the trip will be all expenses paid. I think because of your view against the war, you would be a great candidate to speak at the conference. I am actually against the war too, but it is not an "anti-war" protest—its actually a pro-America peaceful demonstration encouraging us to stand united despite our differing viewpoints.

You have every right to tell the world that you are against the war when you speak and I think that you should. But instead of focusing on that and on how disgusting American politics can be, you should talk about Chris and the life he lived, and what a wonderful young man and husband he was, so that the world will know just what the war took away. If any other war widows are offended by that then they are the ones with the problem and not you—in my opinion.

I would be honored for you to speak "from the heart" about all that you have experienced during this most difficult time for you in hopes that it will help our nation open its eyes more. In a way, this will be an anti-war protest, but it CANNOT be marketed like that, because then we will never be granted the permission to speak.

    Thanks, stay strong and God bless. Lindsey

March 10, 2005. Lavinia's email to her mother-in-law, Vicky Chicoine.

Hi mom,

    Just wanted to send you a quick "I love you." I am missing Cutie very much. 2 more days and I am in the new house. I will leave behind the apartment that Chris and I lived in for two years. I know that Chris will come with me wherever I go, whatever I do. My brother is now trying to get my father's ticket changed so he can leave earlier. I hope he'll succeed in doing so. Which day were you planning on arriving in Portland?

                                         Love you, Lavi

Hi Honey,

    I was planning on 4/21. Jesse will be getting the 20th off, and we need to be together that day. I'm still not sure about asking Grandpa to come with me. We might be restricted on what we do if he comes, however, I would like the company on the drive and I know he would enjoy the trip.

    Jesse took the day off to take Mitch (cucumber dog) to the vet. Mitch has been acting really weird lately, and is having problems with standing. I hope it's not serious. Chris is with you all the time. Sometimes it's not as evident as others, but he's there.

I love you. Mom

March 14, 2005.

Dear Neal,

Lately, I've been mostly sending you group emails. This will end soon when things settle down a bit. I will start to write you personal emails again.

I barely moved in to the house this past Saturday during that stupid snowstorm. I still don't have a phone line and internet cable... As soon as I get settled and I can walk around the house, I'll give you a call and I'll have you and your family come over. Also, I still don't have a car, so it's really hard to get around... I have to depend on rides from friends. It is really difficult. It was a hell to try to move not having my own car...

Hugs, Lavi

At about this time, my then wife, Jill, and now good friend, helped Lavi with shopping transportation. A week or so later, we enjoyed Lavi's company over dinner at our home in Portland.

March 16, 2005. John Gelineau's email to Lavinia.

Dear Lavi,

I just wanted to show you that your message is getting through to people, and that there are people out there who share your ideas. This first letter is from Nancy Robinson. I sent the newspaper article to the Vermont MFSO for distribution. I almost think this is the woman you met on Veterans day in the park, that was so outspoken.

The second letter is from Gretchen Kamilewicz, the woman who sent you the card that I responded to. They obviously received my letter today, and didn't wait to send me this email. I know that you don't like it when people say they are proud of you for speaking out, but I am truly proud to call you my daughter, not because of these letters, but because of your love for Chris.

Love, Dad

March 20, 2005. Denitza Dimitrova's email to Lavinia.

Lavi, I'm sorry to hear about your job and your father coming—how is he doing anyway? Is he back to his "normal" self? Is he coming alone and for what purpose? As far as the ETEP, and your father leaving on the 20th—that date would be symbolic this year, not sad—I think that did happen for a reason. Maybe you will start life anew after that date. Maybe it's time you started living for both Chris and yourself.

You've been through hell this year. I'll keep my fingers crossed for the ETEP program. Although I have so much faith in you, you probably won't need that. :) Congrats about the car. Wish I could be there to help you make your new place feel like home. Love and peace to you, Lavi.

March 23, 2005. Lavinia's group email.

Sorry I have been out of touch… A lot has been going on… Did lots of unpacking. I also had lots of flashbacks. A lot of things reminded me of Chris on Saturday. The smell of the new car made me think of exactly this time a year ago when I purchased the same car with John, my dad-in-law. That morning I talked to Chris on IM and he was really excited for me. I tried to just get my body going, did lots of shopping but that feeling of loss and that distinctive movement in my stomach stayed there the whole day. There was a smell in the air that reminded me of last year.

Maybe it's the smell of spring. On Sunday I had another rough day. Memories of Chris kept popping up everywhere I went. I was in the mall with my mom, eating some Teriyaki chicken (which Chris and I loved to share) and I just thought at one point that if I stretched my hand out, I would reach his hand.

I hate seeing happy people holding hands. I don't hate them: just the fact that I used to love holding hands and now I can't have that. Then, on my way back home I was taking a turn by Best Buy and On the Border (a Mexican restaurant that was our favorite place to celebrate anniversaries and b-days) when Billy Joel's "She's Got a Way About Her" started playing on the radio. About a year ago, more precisely on April 18th (2 days before Chris died) I was taking that exact turn and I was listening to the same song. I had bought that CD from Best Buy and I was planning on using that song in a home-made video with pictures of me, that I would send Chris as a gift for second wedding anniversary. Anyway, it was just weird and it brought tears to my eyes.

I haven't gotten a chance to go and visit Chris lately with the moving process and not having a car. I finally went on Monday. The visit was powerful and overwhelming. So many tears had gathered up inside me and I hadn't even realized that. I held onto Chris' headstone and just let it all come out of me. Sometimes I don't think I even realize how much I miss him.

The shopping excitement is wearing off and I am just heading into a low… As long as I keep spending, I get a fake sense of relief, but spending can't go on forever. I made a budget and I've made sure I stayed within its limits. I like what the house looks like but it just feels empty, empty, empty. Every time I get excited, a feeling of immense sadness counters it, making me experience guilt instead.

Anyway, this is what has happened in life lately.

Peace, Lavi

March 23, 2005. Lavinia's email to Mike Faust.

Hello Mike,

I want to thank you very much for thinking of me and for offering me the archiving job at Central Office. Should the circumstances be different, I would accept the offer in a heartbeat. It is not a matter of me wanting or not wanting to work. Work keeps me busy and helps me maintain my sanity. However, the month of April is the hardest month for me ever. I am already tired and overwhelmed with everything going on lately. A wedding anniversary coming up on April 6th and a year since Chris passed on April 20th are enough to make me unpleasant to be around for anyone… I decided that the month of April will be dedicated to doing something meaningful for me and others, to a higher purpose that Chris would be proud of me undertaking. I will probably do some volunteer relief work at Mercy or at nursing homes around Portland and I will go to VT to be with my dad-in-law and my mom-in-law for awhile. Again, thank you very much. I appreciate your good intentions. Peace, Lavinia

March 24, 2005. Lavinia's email to her mother-in-law, Vicky Chicoine.

Mom,

I had dreams of Chris last night. I am so grateful. I woke up in the morning remembering them clearly, and I kept my eyes closed for another 20 minutes to just enjoy them and make sure I'd remember them later. In the first dream, Chris and I had just met each other, somebody introduced us to each other and he was radiant with joy. The person who introduced us wanted Chris to go somewhere with him but Chris said he doesn't want to go anywhere. He wants to stay with me and get to know me better… I felt like I wanted to hold him, hug him, tell him how much I've missed him, but I could not because it looked like he had just met me for the first time.

The second dream took place somewhere in a park, maybe Cape Elizabeth park where we used to go to often in the summer of 2003. A sunny, marvelous day… Chris was showing/teaching me how to fly a kite that looked like a plane. The kite was flying so high, touching the sky. The sequence to this dream, or maybe it was a totally different dream, was scary. Chris was gone and I could feel that pain in my chest that I experienced after April

20th. Last night I went to bed remembering Chris smiling, laughing, playing with Shushu, driving the Subaru. Then for some reason, I pictured him lying in the casket and the sequence broke. I still don't get how he could be gone... Love, Lavi

Hi Honey.

I'm so glad you had warm, good dreams of Chris. Sometimes, I don't want to wake up because it means facing a world without him. But, I can't hide, I can't sleep away my life—even though Chris is not on this plain of existence any more, he is still around and giving his love and strength any way he can. In dreams, in thoughts, in music, funny hunches, feelings of peace, in tears and hugs shared by all that knew and love him. People still need me, and I can't give up on them—he wouldn't have.

I love you, Mom

March 24, 2005. Lavinia's email to Jessica Bancroft, USM.

Jessica,

I read the online materials on the ETEP website and noticed that April 20th is the date when second round applicants would be selected for any remaining seats.

They also said that second round application screening would take place mid-March. Have interviews already started for second round applicants? I've been so busy lately that I failed to notice we are almost at the end of March.

Thank you, Lavinia

Hi,

> Second round interviews will start soon, so you haven't missed anything yet. You should be hearing from someone maybe next week, or soon thereafter. Jessica

March 28, 2005. Lavinia's email to Kristin Sims.

Hi Kristin,

> I tried to get in touch with you over the weekend and your phone was constantly busy. I have just tried to call you and it did the same thing. Did you guys move out? Let me know when you want to come over to my place to visit and have your paper corrected.
>
> Love, Lavi

On a day in late March, San Pao who had been in the Humvee behind Chris on the convoy, coincidentally pulled up alongside Lavi at a traffic light in Portland. Upon recognizing each other and waiting for the light to turn green, they conversed through the open windows of their cars and agreed to get together some time soon.

In that same general time frame and knowing that her father would be visiting and staying at her house, I called Lavi to ask how things were going and how she was feeling about her father's pending visit. She was quick to express that she understood her father and was confident it would all work out. And she told me that one of her guy friends might be coming over for dinner sometime. I told her that was a good idea.

Having recently returned to Maine with the 133rd, Greg Fiore and Lavi had planned to get together on Friday, April 1, and visit Chris's gravesite at the Evergreen Cemetery. When she failed to show up or confirm, Greg assumed that there was a scheduling misunderstanding or she wasn't ready to meet with him.

IF YOU LOVE SOMEONE, YOU MUST TELL THEM

That same day, April 1, was to be Lavi's last day of work at *Strive*, a nonprofit that helped young adults with emotional and intellectual disabilities. Lavi had decided it was time to move on and pursue her passion to return to the university and earn a master's degree in French and from there, to a career in teaching. Lavi's colleagues at Strive had planned a party for her, but when she failed to show up and aware of her father's visit, they contacted the Westbrook Police Department.

News of Lavi's death sent waves of emotion, grief, and disbelief in Maine and throughout New England and beyond. I was numb with shock having recently chatted with her on the phone, only to pick up the paper with a startling headline of a double death in Westbrook. There are some events in life that hit you so hard, your brain goes into a deep freeze, hibernation. Rage and disbelief followed by tears, hugs, and love are the universal emotions that best express the words we struggle to find.

This tragedy, almost one year since the tragic death of Chris, rattled my awareness that whether we live many years or just a few, our stories are built from one day to the next within the milestones of our cradle to grave calendar. Between those two markers, there is hope that the good and triumphant will outweigh the bad and tragic. But we know and are constantly reminded that life is a fragile gift with no guarantees from one day to the next. The good and the bad are not equally distributed. That is the harsh and unfair reality of life.

The obituaries and profiles of Lavi's life spoke truth to the integrity and nobility of this young woman who grabbed life at both ends, determined to do good for others through learning, empathy, and love. Always the student and teacher, Lavi reached out with passion and honest love to other soldiers and their families, professors at USM, classmates, people who only knew her from the media who flocked to her story, and friends she met along the way.

Maine National Guard and State Family Program director, Staff Sergeant Barbara Claudel, remembered Lavi as someone "who had a great effect on the lives of soldiers and their families even after losing her husband, she kept in constant contact with many soldiers through email and shipped packages overseas to them… A lot of families had a deep connection to her because of the type of person that she was." Lavi was also remembered as attending every funeral of a Maine soldier killed in action. "She was just a great lady, and was doing her best to help everyone out," remembered Major Peter Rogers of the Maine National Guard.

---

[1] Bill Nemitz, "Mosul Suicide Attack Kills 22 including 2 from Maine's 133rd," *Portland Press Herald* (December 21, 2004).
[2] Carter Ham, brigadier general of Task Force Olympia, calling the attack "the worst day of my life." (December 21, 2004).
[3] Alicia Wilkinson's telephone interview with author describing the December 21, 2004, suicide attack in Mosul.
[4] Todd Crawford's email with author detailing the suicide attack and confirming Wilkinson's description.

CHAPTER 11

April 9, 2005: Reunited

THE FUNERAL HAD BEEN SET FOR A week later at the *Woodford Congregational Church* in Portland. I remember it as a warm, sunny, day, yet another April event in the story of Lavinia and Christopher. It was within days of being a full year since Chris had passed. Finding a seat in the balcony, I looked across at the others who sat nearby and gazed down on the crowd below filled with family, friends, classmates, and members of the National Guard. What was happening still seemed impossible to accept and to this day, remains more blur than detail, although I do remember briefly connecting with some of the family of Lavi and Chris after the service.

I also remember what Major Ben Leonard would tell me when I first met him thirteen years later.

Without hesitation, Leonard said, "The most difficult moments in service to the country were folding the flag that was draped over Chris's casket and presenting it to Lavi and one year later, carrying her casket."

In sharing that memory, Leonard also remembers the enduring legacy of Lavi and Chris, "How deeply they were loved by a lot of people, how their spirits are still with us, and it sounds weird, but I still talk with them and feel their spirits."

As reported by the *Boston Globe*, the Reverend Constantine Sarantidis, who had one year earlier presided at Chris's funeral, said he "did not want to dwell on Lavinia Gelineau's death…but about

IF YOU LOVE SOMEONE, YOU MUST TELL THEM

her life, her devotion to helping other grieving military relatives, her wit, and her romantic side."[1]

In remembering Lavinia, Chris's uncle, John Chicoine, said, "The girl had life just blasting out of her all the time, and from the day we met, we already felt like she was part of the family; she fit right in."

Over the year since Chris died, Lavi had met frequently with the chaplain of the Maine National Guard, Andy Gibson. In remembering Chris and Lavi as a couple, Gibson observed, "She felt that the two of them were as one. She more than lost a partner when he died, she lost a part of herself." During the funeral service, Gibson read from Lavi's favorite passages in *The Five People You Meet in Heaven* by Mitch Albom.

The theme of Chris and Lavi's oneness was universal and captured beautifully by Chris's mother, Victoria Chicoine. Her hope was that "the couple will be remembered for what everyone around them saw: uncommon devotion." She added, "I want them to be remembered as having each so much in life that they joined together in death. It was a love everybody dreams of."

Lavi's professor, mentor, and friend, Margaret Reimer, said in an interview, "The Gelineaus' marriage was one of envy, and remembering Lavi hugging Chris's casket, I was looking at what it truly meant to have your heart break."

As reported in the *Boston Globe*, "A touching and memorable moment of the service was captured when Mark Miller strapped on an acoustic guitar and led the mourners in singing *Amazing Grace*, which he had sung with his friend Lavinia Gelineau after her husband had died." Following the song, Miller shared a lesson learned through Lavi when she told him, "Mark, if you love someone, you must tell them. So I repeat to everyone here this morning: If there's someone in your life who you love, you should tell them because tomorrow is not a given. Life is very fragile."

For Lavinia and Chris, the laws of probability and good luck in reaching the age of ninety years would be lost in the heavens, but their expressed self-realization that they were "so lucky…to meet their half" when many never do endures as a lasting truth to the meaning of their lives. May we never forget their legacy of love and giving back to others.

Lavinia was laid to rest alongside Christopher in Portland's Evergreen Cemetery, a National Historic Landmark. Lavi and Chris share the same distinctive red stone that she had commissioned for Chris. They rest together near the tree where Lavi hung chimes to provide music for Chris during the winter months when the song birds had left for their southern homes. Just a few months earlier, Lavi had arranged for a passage of one of her favorite poets, Emily Dickinson, to be chiseled into the stone.

> Not knowing when the dawn will come, I
> open every door.

Honoring Lavinia's deep love of the works of William Shakespeare, the following is offered to her and Chris's memory.

My bounty is as boundless as the sea, My love as deep; the more I give to thee,
The more I have, for both are infinite.
I hear some noise within. Dear love, adieu!
Romeo and Juliet, act 2, scene 11.

Postscript: heading to Romania

With a full and busy life of work and family, it would not be until January of 2018 that I was able to seriously focus on the idea of writing this book. I set aside the self-doubt with a determination to see the project through to the finish.

My plan was to first establish contact with the parents and stepparents of Chris and Lavinia whom I believed were living in Vermont. Knowing that the circle of love between Chris and Lavinia had ironically connected his father, John Gelineau, and her mother, Iulia, it was an easy decision to reach out to them as a logical first step.

It took some time to connect with John, and to my surprise, he and Iulia had moved to Sibiu, Romania, in 2016, from Buxton, Maine, a town just a few miles from my home. So much for my assumption that they were living in Vermont. If I had only known. *But what a unique opportunity*, I thought, *to begin my writing adventure with a journey to the city and country that Lavinia grew up in.*

April 2018
Humberto Delgado Airport, Lisbon, Portugal

I watch the blank faces of my fellow travelers as we shuffle and zigzag the rope line maize, guiding us through airport security. Clutching passports, boarding passes, and carry-on items, we each wait our turn to be cleared for entry to the promised land of the terminal gates and on to wherever the friendly skies are taking us.

Like so many obedient sheep, we have come to accept as the "new normal" all the process and anxiety of air travel. The security protocols confirm the motivation for self-preservation, spawned by the alienated and embittered zealots of fellow human beings.

Moving from one column to the next, my thoughts drift to how we have transformed our interactions with friends, banks, service providers, and just about everyone through usernames and passwords, with each designed to be as unique as the footprints of a newborn. And yet we have come to learn that our efforts at secrecy are imperfect at best. We remain vulnerable to the few who will do all they can, whether by deceit, technology, or even force, to cash in on the many.

The mind-numbing trance of air travel precipitates more reflection with the realization that behind each unknown face, there is a story that begins the same way. We were all born into the world through the coming together of thousands of generations, each at very precise moments as determined through circumstances and chance encounters. That is a miracle we all share regardless of race, ethnicity, or religion.

No matter how many days and years we have, no one is excluded from the chain of life. There is no test of good or evil or wealth or poverty or political preference. While some of us are the product of planning, others an unintended consequence, we are all in the chain. And for all of us, our lives and the lives of all living matter are circles with a beginning and end. The arc of some circles is wider than others, but each is a clean and exact 360 degrees.

Walking to my gate of departure through a cleverly designed trail of duty-free shops, I continued to focus on my fellow travelers as we streamed past each other. Where are they coming from, and where are they are going? Are they so caught up in their own lives that they're not paying attention? No doubt, some are looking at me the same way. Like riding a subway, eye contact is conducted discretely, if at all. While many will be reuniting with family, friends, and business associates, others are moving on to a new chapter that will carry them to the far reaches from where they started.

The excitement of these new pioneers, the ones who are turning the page to a new chapter, is one of nervous anticipation of the unknown challenges and hoped for rewards that await their fresh start. They have weighed the pros and cons of a bold move and have reached a comfort zone to shoot for the stars. The path to a new life—be it by land, sea, or in more recent times, flying like an eagle, high above land and sea—has motivated the human species to look beyond the horizon, to dream and wonder what the other side of the mountain looks like. And now the search for the other side has broadened its scope to look deep beyond the stars. But I'll leave the details of that one for my grandchildren to figure out.

No wonder that the lure of moving on, the yearning for change, often results in meeting one's other half. Such were the different paths that brought Chris Gelineau from Vermont and Lavinia Onitiu from Romania to the University of Southern Maine in Portland. In that city by the sea, they met, fell in love, got married, and shared dreams of a long future together as husband and wife.

As I navigated through security, my trip to Sibiu was a reminder that in life, one thing leads to another. Case in point, the new security protocols are a direct response to September 11, 2001, and how the horror and tragedy of that day triggered a chain reaction of events that seventeen years later, motivated me to travel to Romania.

My flight out of Lisbon brought me to Vienna, where I changed from a new and very comfortable three-hundred-passenger Airbus to a narrow and noisy twenty-passenger turbo prop for the ninety-minute leg to the City of Sibiu. It was a classic early spring afternoon, another April day no less, sunny and warm with nice views out to the Eastern European countryside.

As the plane drew closer to Sibiu, my thoughts turned to Lavinia and the excitement she must have felt while heading to America for the first time. She had won a scholarship to study in America and was moving forward with a new chapter that would carry her to the far reaches from where she started.

After a few weeks of exchanging emails with John Gelineau, I was in airspace over Romania and the plane was now in its final approach to the Aeroportul International Sibiu. Although the airport underwent an upgrade in 2008, it nonetheless had a tired look and feel, kind of a hangover from its many years under the communist military rule that finally ended in a revolution in 1989. The block letters, spelling the airports name, stood like giant toy soldiers at rigid attention on the terminal roof, reminding me of the Soviet-era airport in Barnaul, a city in the Siberian region of Russia that I had traveled to in 1995, four years after Russia and the other republics of the Soviet Union became sovereign nations.

I returned to Maine from that trip with an adopted young daughter to join our family. Fortunately, I had the good sense to maintain a journal throughout that transformative journey. Trust me, there were a number of never-to-be-experienced-again moments from start to finish. Moments consumed with anxiety, others with humor and more with the insights gained when we travel to other nations and cultures.

One experience of the special-moment kind occurred on the return flight to America. As the Russian Aeroflot plane entered American airspace and prepared to land in New York, the pilot welcomed the passengers, most of whom were Russian, to the United States of America. His message was met with instantaneous applause and cheering, leaving me with goosebumps and a sense that good things in the world were happening. Russia was shedding its Soviet Union coat and moving in a more open and positive direction. There was hope and a sense of a new world order. Unfortunately, with Vladimir Putin's rise to power in the late 90s, it was short-lived.

Circling back to my trip to Romania, passengers disembarked on the tarmac. Once through customs, I anxiously scanned the reception area for John. He, of course, was looking for me, and the body language of two people looking for each other quickly connected us. I would spend the next few days almost exclusively with John and Iulia who were warm and generous hosts, providing me with a wonderful apartment and exceptional home and restaurant cuisine.

Apparently, I was the first American to visit John and Iulia since their move to Romania in 2016. In a reversal of America's history as a welcoming beacon for millions who seek a new start, John and Iulia came to realize that their retirement years would be working years. Lacking a significant pension and faced with high health insurance costs, it was John who suggested the move from America to Romania. He explained, "With rents of $200 per month and very low health insurance expense because Romania provides universal health insurance. One can live comfortably on monthly social security income of $1,000."

At the suggestion of Iulia's son, Marius, they gradually purchased four apartments, one of which they live in and the others they rent. As described by John, that additional income stream allows them "to do what we want and when we want, and if we need more money, we can sell one or more of the apartments because the city is growing." In fact, before this book is published, John and Iulia will have moved to a new single-family house currently under construction. In the years since my trip to Sibiu, John has found his creative side with paintings that are colorful, imaginative, and of remarkable quality.

With a population close to 150,000, the City of Sibiu is located in the Transylvania Region of Romania. Framed by the Fagaras Mountains, which are part of the Carpathian Mountain Chain and straddled by the River Olt, a tributary of the famous Danube River, the first official records of Sibiu date back to the late twelfth century and the arrival of settlers from Germany who were known as Transylvanian Saxons.

Over the ensuing years, the city would grow to be one of the largest and wealthiest walled cities of the Medieval Era. Significant sections of the massive defensive walls and towers remain today and help frame the centuries-old medieval squares that further define the historic center of the city. Together with its numerous churches and places of worship, Sibiu was recognized for centuries for its religious tolerance and today is considered a vital European cultural center.

Walking is the very best way to see a city, to feel its pulse and character, study the architecture, discover the little nooks and crannies, and watch and learn from the people who live there. Because of the numerous stops and unseasonably high temperature, John and Iulia wisely mapped out an itinerary that combined driving and walking.

Our travels brought us to the neighborhood surrounding the large apartment building that Lavi's family lived in for many years. Located at the corner of a busy intersection, the multistory building was another reminder of the heavy block, cold architecture I had seen in Russia. Unlike the years that Lavi's family lived there, the parking lots today are filled with cars, further evidence of a broader and stronger consumer-based economy.

One night over dinner at their home, I learned that under Romania's OUI laws, a blood alcohol level above 0.0 is considered a criminal offense and automatic loss of one's driving license. Similarly strict is the process for purchasing a gun. It includes training, psychological evaluations, waiting periods, and background checks. In 2018, a total of twenty-seven people died from firearms. Nonetheless, parts of Romania, including the Carpathian mountains, are popular destinations for wild game hunting.

I tried to imagine what life must have been like under communist rule and particularly during Lavi's early years. Iulia shared that from the second to fourth grade, Lavi wore the "young Pioneer" uniform every day to school. The Pioneers was an initiative of Romania's communist party that included a standard uniform for youth and directed by the Central Committee of the Romanian Communist Party.

A visit to the church where Lavi was baptized and where she and Chris were married was made all the more real by a baptism of a young child that was in progress as we arrived. Iulia explained that the practicing of religion under communism was made difficult by the heavy hand of the party leaders and the overreach of the state. During the dark days of communist rule, churches that were not destroyed stood as powerful and enduring symbols of hope for a better day.

By most measures, the Romania of today is a far different place from it was in 1979, the year Lavinia was born. Her first ten years, all of which were in Sibiu, were spent under the last ten years of Nicolae Ceausescu's harsh, cruel communist regime. With his wife, Elena, Ceausescu had come to power as the general secretary of the Romania Communist Party in 1964.

According to Iulia, the early years of his regime were relatively stable with decent jobs and sufficient necessities of life. That stability was short lived as widespread shortages of food, including, at times, long lines for milk and other necessities, became the roller-coaster ride of life for Romanians.

If scrounging for food wasn't bad enough, Ceausescu's arrogant and cruel mismanagement of the economy was made all the worse through his deliberate rationing of electricity, gas, and water. In the September 1, 2015, issue of the *Economist,* under the story line, *Remembering life in Romania under communist rule,* "In winter the average temperature inside a Bucharest apartment dropped to eight degrees." Put another way, Ceausescu committed genocide through the deliberate starvation and freezing of innocent human beings.

That same article speaks to how the United States in the 1970s, a time still dominated by Cold War politics, was "impressed with Ceausescu's political distance from the Soviet Union and his protest against the Soviet invasion of Czechoslovakia in 1968." Consequently, and according to the *Economist* article, American policy shifted to allow Romania to borrow money at low interest rates.

Unfortunately, opening that door was like giving a teenager their first credit card with no supervision. Ceausescu proceeded to spend way beyond his means and with great extravagance. To meet the bulging and ever-expanding debt, Ceausescu ordered a policy of mass export of natural resources and goods and services, thereby leaving the people starved, frozen, and demoralized, all the while massaging his ego with glitz, huge parades, and showmanship.

Applying the cruel template of fascist dictator, and strong-arm leaders, Ceausescu amassed his power through the cultivation of Big Brother fear and intimidation. His secret police, the *Securitate*, evolved in to "one of the Eastern Bloc's largest and most feared secret police forces." Only state news was allowed. Individuals caught listening to outside news could be arrested if caught. Responding to tattletale informants and supposed friends, thousands of citizens were hauled away in the darkness of night.

Many of the victims would tragically end up in Sighet with most over the age of sixty. It hardly seems coincidental that Ceausescu's choice of Sighet was also the home to thousands of Jews who were sent to their death in Auschwitz and Buchenwald during World War II. Among the survivors was Elie Wiesel and two of his three sisters. For his lifework illuminating the horrors of the Nazi's, Weisel was awarded a *Nobel Peace Prize* in 1986. In presenting the award, Wiesel was recognized "for being a messenger to mankind: His message is one of peace, atonement, and dignity."

In stark contrast to Wiesel's message of humanity, the chilling message of Ceausescu's use of Sighet is memorialized on a plaque at the entrance to the museum in that city: "The greatest victory of communism was to create people without a memory, a brainwashed new man unable to remember what he was, what he had, or what he did before communism."

There is a judgment day, a day of reckoning, and when so many suffer and for so long, the final chapter of many a dictator often plays out through violence. The people rise up and finally say, "Enough is enough." Such was the case in Romania with protests in 1989 that first erupted in the City of Timisoara during a speech that Ceausescu was giving to thousands of Romanians. In the immediate days following, revolution swept across Romania with hundreds of citizens killed. For Ceausescu's troops, this was the last straw; and rather than continuing to kill their fellow citizens, they joined with them in the battle to move their country to a more open and free nation.

Iulia remembers those days of violence and uncertainty and how her family remained in their apartment to the sound of nearby gunfire. She described "big fighting in the city square involving protestors, police and the military, with many shot."

Ceausescu and his wife, Elena, attempted to flee the country, but their effort was thwarted by the very army that kept him power. Following a nationally televised trial, they were both tried and found guilty of murder and on that same day, publicly killed by firing squad. It was Christmas Day, and the people celebrated as the *iron curtain* of the Ceausescu era fell from its grip. Replacing the dark clouds was the optimistic hope for a future of freedom and opportunity.

Throughout my stay in Sibiu, conversations with Iulia and John covered a range of topics, from the personal to the political, including the continued distrust of Russia. We shared a natural back-and-forth that provided a relaxed and respectful setting for remembering Lavi and Chris and the gift of their contagious personalities. One night following dinner, photo albums and Lavi's two *magna cum laude* diplomas were brought out. What an affirmation of her commitment to shoot for the stars, which her mother inspired in her.

I learned that on the anniversary of each death, a candle is lit in their honor and remains burning the entire day, followed by a family dinner that continues a cultural tradition of giving food to others. Toward the end of my visit, John was tired, so Iulia and I went for a quiet early evening walk. The subject of Lavi's love of learning surfaced again and how her academic excellence opened the door to a full scholarship and opportunity to build a future in America. Iulia reinforced how that was exactly what Lavi wanted. She loved living in the United States and was committed to making it her permanent home.

In expressing her enormous pride for Lavi's accomplishments, Iulia openly acknowledged the unintended consequences that resulted from a random seating arrangement at an academic conference. Our conversation carried that theme to the uncertainty of each day and the hard truth that only when all the steps have been taken will each of our paths be memorialized.

Reflecting back to my conversation that night with Iulia, I am struck by the realization that the underlying theme of unintended consequences as applied to Lavi and Chris has ironically drawn me to its web of unintended consequences.

The story of these two beautiful young people doing good for others and brimming with life and love, only to be trapped within the prism of war and violence, proved personally overwhelming. That narrative, in combination with personal life-transition challenges, the poisonous politics of a pandemic, and the increasingly loud and deeply divided America, contributed to my random debilitating panic attacks.

Drawing from Lavi's look into the mirror, when she rhetorically asked, "Where are you going, girl?" I did likewise and decided to seek professional counseling through cognitive behavioral therapy (CBT). I encourage others to seek help when they feel lost and overwhelmed. It's entirely human. Think of it this way. If you break your leg, everyone can see it and will shower you with sympathy. If the fight is entrenched within, it will remain hidden within until one decides to deal with their demons and shortcomings. Fortunately, attitudes are changing, but generations-long stigmas can have a long shelf life.

Let me be clear. The impact of their story is not to compare my experience with those who served with Chris in Iraq or the personal pain of the families and loved ones who lived each day with the anxiety and fear of what might be happening all those miles away. But it does offer a glimpse of understanding as to why many soldiers and first responders carry deep psychological scars and emotional pains, often diagnosed as post-traumatic stress disorder (PTSD).

Toward the end of my visit to Sibiu, the obvious signs of a changing country governed through a democratic parliamentary system and driven by a diverse economy tethered to the European Union were reinforced in a different way. From the modern highrise apartment that I was staying in, the view out included farmland, precisely at the edge of the most recent development.

That visual was juxtaposed with a shepherd managing his flock a few hundred yards beyond the development. He was a link to the chain of countless others who, over the many decades and centuries, made a living from those fields. Distance wise, that field was not far from the walls of the old city, but in many ways, it was light-years beyond. I thought, *How many years or even months before that field is gone and with it, a piece of a different economy, a different life?*

Thus, there are two sides to a coin, and the local, regional, and global challenge is to keep plowing ahead, like a farmer in the field, committed to a sustainable tomorrow that honors the past while requiring fairness, compassion, and best practices today. Ultimately, there are trade-offs, a reality I learned through a lengthy professional career of public service management working for elected boards of directors, often involving highly contentious public projects and issues.

With that perspective, a poignant sign of Sibiu's new economy and expanding middle class was captured in the window of the adjacent apartment building to where I was staying. The light of day was passing through a handmade sign that was taped to the window. Backward, the letters in English spelled, "I love [a brilliant red heart] my home."

That simple message conveyed the universal desire for a home to call your own—a place where your heart is. I wondered who that person or persons might be if a couple like Chris and Lavi—how did they meet? What were the personal decisions and the decisions of others that impacted their lives? What were the unintended consequences, either good or bad, that shaped their story?

As I reflected on these questions, my mind flashed back to the last time I saw Lavinia and Chris as a couple. We were at a busy intersection in Portland, near the USM campus. I had stopped at a red light and was waiting for it to turn green. They didn't see me as their focus was entirely on each other. They stood arm and arm, also waiting for the light to change, laughing with their equally infectious smiles. It was all very human, very real, and they were obviously very much in love.

---

[1] Michael Levenson, "Now family grieves for a young widow," *Globe Correspondent* (archive.boston.com, April 10, 2005).

Notes and Sources

SOURCES FOR MUCH OF THE MATERIAL IN this book derive from my personal communications with the many individuals whom I interviewed. Consequently, some attributions are embedded in the manuscript through standard quotation marks and by direct reference to the source, be it a soldier, family member, author, or journalist.

A significant source of information is the emails of Lavinia Gelineau and a flash drive containing Lavinia's emails that her father-in-law, John Gelineau, provided to me. Lavinia's emails are uniquely important to preserving her and Chris Gelineau's legacy. I was deliberate in selecting emails that in my judgment added value and context to the story while minimizing the potential to tilt too far in what should remain respectful of Lavi, Chris, and their families. Whether I achieved the desired balance I will leave to the judgment of others. I did my best.

While the media stories are a matter of public record, the chore of tracking down the most relevant to the story was made easier through the kindness of Lieutenant Colonel Chris Elgee, who loaned me his extensive collection of the *Portland Press Herald* and *Maine Sunday Telegram* coverage of the 133rd Engineering Battalion's deployment to Iraq.

The bibliography and other key sources of information that helped in writing the story are listed below.

Bibliography

Allen, Thomas. *Dangerous Convictions: What's Really Wrong with the U.S. Congress.* New York and Oxford University Press, 2013.

Barton, Frederick. *Peace Works: America's Unifying Role in a Turbulent World.* Rowman & Littlefield Publishing Group, Inc. Lanham, Maryland, 2018.

Bush, George W. *Decision Points.* Crown Publishing Group, a division of Random House, Inc. New York, 2012.

Clarke, Richard A. *Against All Enemies: Inside America's War on Terror.* Free Press, a division of Simon & Schuster, Inc. New York, New York, 2004.

Griffith, W. Zach. *Packed for the Wrong Trip: A New Look Inside Abu Ghraib and the Citizen-Soldiers Who Redeemed America's Honor.* Arcade Publishing, New York, New York, 2016

Maddox, Eric. *Mission: Black List #1: The Inside Story of the Search for Saddam Hussein—As Told by the Soldier Who Masterminded His Capture.* Harper Collins Publishers, New York, New York, 2008.

Moore, Michael. *Will They Ever Trust Us Again? Letters from the War Zone.* Published by the Penguin Group, London, England, and New York, New York, 2004.

Acknowledgments

Taking on the challenge of writing this book was a journey I never imagined, but here I am, composing a thank-you for the tremendous support and encouragement so many have extended my way. I accept those good feelings as they confirm the place in our hearts that Lavi and Chris will forever hold. The privilege of their companionship and friendship during the time they walked with us will always stay with us. Together, they represent the best of humanity.

However this book may be received, I know that I gave it my all, just as the soldiers of the 133rd did during their time in Iraq. The support and encouragement of retired Major General Bill Libby and retired Colonel John Jansen provided me with the confidence to reach out to many others in the battalion. The time and support extended to me by so many was humbling, and all the more moving, with soldiers who were directly involved in the tragedies of April 20, 2004 and December 21, 2004. Lavi's professor, mentor, and close friend, Dr. Margaret Reimer, along with close friends, Denitza Dimitrova and Leslie and Travis Scribner, provided long and wonderful insights and memories of their relationships with Lavi and Chris. Raye-Lynn Jansen and my friend, Deborah, provided an important critical eye at key moments in my writing process. A special thanks to Kelly Crum of Page Publishing for her consistent patience and support of the many changes I made during the writing of this book. Without the support and constructive input of John Gelineau, it would have been nearly impossible to write this book. He and the other family members of Chris and Lavi, most notably, Vicky Chicoine, and lulia Gelineau, are an inspiration. Thank you all and thank you to the many others along the way for your friendship and support.

About the Author

WHILE HIS MAINE ROOTS ARE DEEP, NEAL Allen spent his youth in Upstate New York. His career of public service includes leadership positions at the municipal, regional, and state levels. He was assistant city manager and acting city manager for the city of Portland and, for eighteen years, served as the executive director of the Greater Portland Council of Governments and the Southern Maine Economic Development District. On separate occasions, Allen was the executive director of two regional solid waste management corporations, guiding each through the challenges of development and program implementation. At the state level, he served as the Maine Governor's liaison to the National Governors Association. A veteran of the Coast Guard. Allen has continued his commitment to community service through active participation on housing and education boards.

Printed in the USA
CPSIA information can be obtained
at www.ICGtesting.com
LVHW052142130324
774241LV00020B/298

9 798887 930480